RECONNECTING DETACHED YOUTH WORK
GUIDELINES AND STANDARDS FOR EXCELLENCE

RECONNECTING DETACHED YOUTH WORK
GUIDELINES AND STANDARDS FOR EXCELLENCE

Graeme A. Tiffany

Acknowledgements

I would like to thank members of the project's steering group for their support and critical engagement with the many issues that emerged through the research. They were Tracy Brown, Terry Cane, Bernard Davies, Trevor Gabriel, Tony Jeffs, Sue Houlton, Jon Niblo, David Whewell and Helen White.

Thanks also to the many detached youth workers, managers and other officers of the following partner agencies:

- Blackpool Borough Council Youth Service
- London Borough of Camden Youth and Connexions Service, in particular the Camden Detached Project
- Kent County Council Youth and Community
- Nottingham City Youth Service
- Sheffield Futures
- Tameside Metropolitan Borough Council Youth Service, in particular the Tameside Youth Detached Service (TYDS)
- Worcestershire County Council Youthworcs. Education Directorate

These agencies also helped me to reach young people and the representatives of communities and organisations (both statutory and voluntary) working in partnership with detached youth workers.

I am grateful to Anfield Detached Youth Work Project in Liverpool for permission to use their image on the front cover and the staff of RPM Print and Design for refashioning it in a way that evokes the significance of 'Reconnecting'.

The Federation for Detached Youth Work (FDYW), who commissioned this research, would like to thank Terry Cane for the work he did in envisioning and supporting this project and the contribution he made to securing funds though the National Youth Agency's Partners in Innovation scheme. The 'Fed' is grateful to the NYA for funding and supporting this work.

The views expressed in Reconnecting Detached Youth Work are mine. They are supported by the Federation for Detached Youth Work but are not necessarily those of the NYA.

Graeme A. Tiffany

About the author

Graeme Tiffany is a freelance researcher, trainer and consultant in youth and community work. He specialises in the use of philosophical tools that promote learning and support wider participation in decision-making. Graeme worked for many years as a detached youth worker. He is the author of a number of articles and papers on detached youth work and is a regular contributor at conferences both at home and abroad on this theme.

First published in 2007 by
The Federation for Detached Youth Work

Copyright © The Federation for Detached Youth Work

The right of Graeme A. Tiffany to be identified as the author of this work has been asserted by him in accordance with the Copyright, Designs and Patents Act 1988.

All rights reserved. No part of this publication may be reproduced, stored in a retrieval system, or transmitted, in any form or by any means, without prior written permission of the publisher, nor be otherwise circulated in any form of binding or cover other than that which it is published and without a similar condition including this condition being imposed on the subsequent purchaser.

ISBN: 9780955729607

Cover design by RPM Print & Design

Printed and bound in Great Britain by
RPM Print & Design
2-3 Spur Road, Chichester, West Sussex, PO19 8PR

CONTENTS

BACKGROUND TO THE PROJECT — 1
The *Partners in Innovation* (PIN) scheme — 1
Context of the application by the Federation for Detached Youth Work — 1
Methodology — 3

WHAT IS DETACHED YOUTH WORK? — 4
Youth Work — 4
What differentiates detached youth work from other forms of youth work? — 4
Caveats — 6
What is *not* detached youth work, and why? — 7
A historical analysis of detached youth work — 8
Towards an authentic definition — 9
The aims of detached youth work — 9

FINDINGS & ANALYSIS — 11
The identity of detached youth work — 11
Observations of practice — 12
Related analysis — 13
Why do detached youth work? Moving away from detached youth work as a default option — 16
Where do detached youth workers work? The importance of assessing need — 18
Community profiling — 20
Who should detached youth workers be working with? — 21
Contact making/The significance of street-based contact — 23
The importance of relationships — 24
Process or programme? Detached youth workers or detached teachers? — 25
Reflection, Reviewing and Analysis: The centrality of good judgement-making — 29
How long and how often should detached youth workers work with young people? — 30
Tackling the bureaucracy burden: monitoring, targets, recording and accrediting outcomes versus evaluation and evidence-gathering: the case for focussing on the assessment of learning — 32
Political dimensions of detached youth work: the significance of participation and advocacy — 34
Promotion — 35
Infrastructure: Base and administrative support — 36

CONTENTS

Funding	37
Management	39
Staffing	40
'Fit'	42
Partnership working (detached youth work perspective)	42
Partnership working: partners' perspective	43
Training	45

WIDER CONTEXTUAL ISSUES — 48

Social policy context	48
The importance of professional autonomy	49
Does process-oriented work face extinction?	50
Internalisation	50
Social exclusion	51

ENDPIECE — 52

References — 54

Appendix 1: The history of detached youth work — 56

Appendix 2: Key Guidelines and Standards for Excellence — 58

BACKGROUND TO THE PROJECT

The *Partners in Innovation* (PIN) scheme

In 2005, The National Youth Agency (NYA) commissioned a number of projects to support youth work. Funded by the Local Government Association (LGA), the PIN scheme sought innovative and developmental projects around the following themes:

- young people's health, well-being and safety in the community;
- the contribution of youth work to wider services for young people;
- youth arts as a vehicle for young people's voice in the community;
- the role of young people in performance management and quality assurance in services for young people.

Context of the application by the Federation for Detached Youth Work

The Federation for Detached Youth Work (FDYW) is a voluntary organisation set up and run by a voluntary executive committee comprised of detached youth workers and others working in the field of detached youth work. Its aim is to support detached youth workers, improve practice and promote a wider understanding of what detached youth work is and the values that underpin it. Thus it promotes the development of detached youth work nationally.

The FDYW played a significant role in the Joseph Rowntree Foundation (JRF)-funded research *Reaching Socially Excluded Young People: A national study of street-based youth work* (2004). This study identified the very real contribution that street-based youth work makes in supporting young people out of social exclusion. The study did, though, show that street-based youth work exists in many forms, has no consistent pattern and varies in quality. The FDYW recognised that the PIN scheme represented an opportunity to affirm and detail what detached youth work (as distinct from street-based youth work) is and, indeed, what it looks like when excellent.

In 2005, the FDYW was commissioned under the theme of *The contribution of youth work to wider services for young people* to formulate guidelines and standards for excellence in detached youth work.

A note about the concept of standards:

Standard: *thing against which something may be compared for testing or measurement; required level of quality of proficiency*

Standards increasingly shape the learning experience of young people. This applies as much to youth work as it does to schools, colleges and other educational arenas. Detached youth work has not been exempt from this. Developing standards for excellence in detached youth work is challenging, not least because of the problems inherent in the language of standards and excellence.

Standards are the benchmarks by which performance is judged and evaluated. Standards cannot be raised (as is implied in the rhetoric of 'raising standards'). Rather, it is performance against these standards that changes (it can go both up and down). And so does our sense of what is good. Therein a standard is not raised but changed. People can perform better, but if the standard is set higher they will be deemed to have failed. Excellence implies *of the highest order* and, by implication, it is rarely achieved.

Making sense of this depends on an understanding of values. Values are based on judgements. In this case, about the kind of knowledge, skills and attitudes we should expect to see within excellent detached youth work. But this is not a done deal:

Intrinsic to the understanding of standards whereby performance is to be judged are the values to which the notion of standards are logically linked. Standards are not self-evident because the values they embody are rarely self-evident or beyond dispute.

(Pring, 2005:37)

Clearly there are (and probably always will be) different understandings of what constitutes 'excellent detached youth work', albeit that the current Ofsted framework – see Butler (2005) is, necessarily, the current standard against which youth services are judged.

Meaningful research into excellence must not therefore be bound by a narrow view determined by the current position on what is good. It must explore different understandings and, more fundamentally, scrutinise the values that inform them. Only then can such research identify an ethically defensible set of aims. These are set out below.

This research finds that excellence in detached youth work has more to do with the professional judgement and values of detached youth workers than a set of prescribed standards. So, a series of **guidelines** is also offered to support the thinking and judgement–making that this implies.

It is reasonable, though, to expect all those whose aim it is to provide excellent detached youth work to commit to all the standards and guidelines, not to just a few. These should help projects, support assessment of current practice and inform changes needed to improve the quality and effectiveness of detached youth work.

Methodology

Eight partner agencies were chosen for this research, which took place in 2006. They represent the diversity of environments in which detached youth work can be found. They include a broad scope of detached youth work in rural, inner and outer city settings and administered by local and unitary authorities, county councils and by an agency that had been commissioned by a city council to run youth services.

The research used a conversation-based methodology to explore the opinions of detached youth workers, their managers, other partners and the young people they work with. Discussions centred on the factors that contribute to and detract from the practice of excellence. Its emphasis was on the 'real world' and voice of detached youth work. The research aimed to identify both the features of good practice and any barriers to it.

Questions were based on the following themes, which a literature review revealed to be important in informing the quality of detached youth work:

— aims, values and standards;
— theory, practice and curriculum;
— policies, guidelines and legal imperatives;
— demands and drivers;
— procedures, planning and service development;
— funding and resources;
— staffing, training and development;
— management, supervision and support;
— monitoring and evaluation;
— partnership and participation;
— community and promotion.

Guideline:
- **These themes should be used to assess the rationale behind new projects and the quality of existing provision. They represent a checklist for all involved in detached youth work. See Appendix 2.**

WHAT IS DETACHED YOUTH WORK?

Determining guidelines and standards for excellence in detached youth work calls for a robust definition of detached youth work.

In defining detached youth work, this study aims to:
- explore the value base of youth work;
- consider what is distinctive about detached youth work;
- offer a historical analysis of detached youth work and how this has shaped its aims and values.

This will identify the features of an authentic, value-based definition of detached youth work. As will be shown, this definition, clearly presented, has a positive impact on all aspects of detached youth work.

Youth work:

- Has an emphasis on relationships, as defined by young people. These include young people's relationships with youth workers and with their own peers, social groups and communities. This emphasis implies working with young people as people and not as problems.
- Starts from young people's perspective (the ways of understanding the world that *they* bring and the benefits *they* ascribe to their involvement); it puts them at the centre of a process that they own. Workers show respect for young people's power and control over their own lives, and negotiate with them how they want to be involved, what issues they want to explore and what needs they want to be met.
- Emerges from the conversations of young people and a dialogue with workers. Thereafter, it enables young people to be heard and helps them to influence decision-making at various levels.
- Provides young people with opportunities and support for their personal and social development. It challenges young people to participate in new activities and experiences, thereby broadening their horizons.
- Its purpose [also] is to promote the welfare of young people through *'intervention and prevention' to address the individual institutional and policy causes of disaffection and exclusion* (DfEE., 2001). Intervention includes advocating on behalf of young people.

What differentiates detached youth work from other forms of youth work?

Detached youth work is not unique; it has all the characteristics of generic youth work. A number of these characteristics are, though, thrown into much sharper focus. These relate to issues of power, authority and control. What sets detached youth work apart is its willingness to negotiate on these issues *and* on where it takes place. This is why some young people are prepared to engage with detached youth workers and no others.

Territory

All youth work seeks to work on and from young people's 'territory' (as determined by *their* definitions of space, needs, interests, concerns and lifestyles). Detached youth work, however, is distinct from all other forms of youth work as this concept of territory focuses primarily on the geographical: detached youth workers work *where* young people have chosen to be, whether this be on streets, in cafés, in shopping centres etc.

Young person: "Detached youth workers are different because they come to us."

Flexibility

Detached youth work is, above all, about working flexibly. Detached youth workers don't have to look after buildings. They can therefore use their geographical flexibility to best meet the needs of young people. They celebrate the uncertainty implied by an open-ended way of working and value this for its democratic credentials. They recognise its effectiveness in engaging, in particular, those young people whose lifestyles are sometimes chaotic and sit uncomfortably with order and prescription:

Effective face-to-face work appears to require greater scope for discretion, negotiation and innovation …
Crimmens et al., 2004:74

Agenda

Historically, the earliest attempts to engage young people on the street were made by social scientists, using a questioning approach. This was seen by both parties to have educational value. By trying to understand the lives of young people without imposing any pre-set agenda, social scientists managed to establish relationships with disengaged young people. This Socratic style has underpinned the work of many who recognise that it offers a potential for learning far greater than one with a pre-set agenda.

Young people's principal agenda is, invariably, socially oriented. They engage with the youth service because it is something they want to do in their leisure time. So it represents an environment in which they can socialise with friends and meet new people. Requests for support almost always emerge from this context. Historically, youth work has avoided attempts to drive through a pre-determined agenda as this would contradict its commitment to negotiation and the democratic rights of young people to control what they do in their free time. And anyway, it rarely works: the experience of many detached youth workers is that imposing an agenda acts as a barrier to working with young people, many of whom are already disengaged from formal learning.

The success of youth work comes from making good judgements in relation to these risks. Pushing too hard can distance young people. Not pushing enough can fail to challenge and inspire them. The agenda must, therefore, emerge from a mutually respectful relationship, where hearing the other's voice is as important as articulating one's own. The concept of negotiation seems to embody this; it does not suggest control, domination or licence. It accords instead status to both parties and value to their opinions. A consensus thus emerges.

Neighbourhood and community development

Compared to their centre-based colleagues, detached youth workers spend more time on the streets of local communities. They come face-to-face with the vagaries of community life on a daily basis. Engaging with the community is intrinsic to their work and implies a commitment to involvement in neighbourhood and community development.

Detached youth workers work with community involvement structures on neighbourhood development that benefits young people. Detached youth work aims to provide an active political presence and to support young people's participation in decision-making systems as part of their political education – by helping them have a voice in neighbourhood forums, for example.

In development terms, detached youth work also helps young people access other elements of the wider youth service. It works with them to remove any barriers to such opportunities.

Caveats

Voluntary association

Detached youth work depends absolutely on young people's voluntary association. By contrast, building-based youth services require young people to give up at least some of this voluntary characteristic. Effectively, they enter into an agreement to abide by the constraints placed upon them. The **boundaries** of centre-based work are drawn much more tightly than for detached youth work. It is precisely this lack of constraints that draws some young people to detached youth workers rather than to centre-based workers.

In young people's leisure time

Youth work takes place in young people's leisure time. Detached youth workers might, by contrast, work legitimately in school time with young people who are absent (including unauthorised) or excluded from school. [Note: this definition calls in to question the validity of the description 'school-based youth work'. Ostensibly, this practice employs youth work **methodology** as distinct from being youth work as such.]

Group work

Detached youth work emphasises a group context (that of young people's *existing* group relationships and interactions) more than do other forms of youth work. In detached youth work, young people set the group / social context. In centre-based youth work, (although young people may attend as groups), the centre sets the social context.

Accessibility

Centre-based youth work sometimes depends on young people agreeing to participate in pre-arranged activities. It may not be possible, for example, for a young person to access provision once a project is already underway. Detached youth work's presence on the streets makes this kind of discrimination impossible, even if a particular piece of work is ongoing. Detached youth workers are therefore always accessible to both young people and to the wider community. This adds to the greater emphasis on neighbourhood development and a responsibility to advocate on behalf of young people.

Detached youth workers are acutely aware that they inhabit a space in which young people often test the boundaries associated with the mores and norms of their local communities and wider society. It tries to offer a medium in which young people can do this positively.

What is *not* detached *youth* work, and why?

This research identified a range of practices described as 'detached youth work'. Many, though, don't meet the definitions of detached youth work described above.

Detached work and detached youth work: a necessary distinction for excellence

This project puts detached youth work squarely within the wider context of youth work. Work with young people in a detached setting is not necessarily detached youth work.

Making this distinction is important, as there are ever increasing attempts to work with young people on the street and in non-building based environments. In the words of one detached youth worker:

"Just because someone is working on the street with young people doesn't make it detached youth work."

Outreach is not detached youth work

Put simply, outreach work involves *reaching out*, with a view to coaxing people into a service or provision. Outreach often takes place from a centre or building-based project. It will, initially, aim to provide those contacted with information about services and provision. Outreach workers might work with young people in the settings in which they contact them. This will, usually though, be a short-lived step towards bringing them in, or back in, to that service. A mobile facility such as a bus is sometimes used to support outreach.

Outreach workers may also take a service out to those who don't otherwise use it, without obligation to use building-based services thereafter. Outreach workers often work in town centres where there is no discernible local community and populations are highly transient.

In addition, outreach can be issue-based:

Outreach work may also aim to draw certain identified groups or individuals such as young opiate users or prolific young offenders, into building-based services in which more tightly structured work can take place.
Crimmens et al., 2004:14

By contrast, detached youth work seeks to work in a local community context, with young people in settings of their choice and without a particular service orientation.

Mobile is not detached youth work

Mobile provision is most commonly 'vehicle-based' youth work (Davies, 2001). The vehicle, in essence, acts as a mobile youth club or a mechanism for *outreach*.

Detached youth work (by the definition used in this report) has a long history of using vehicles – for example, vans to transport sporting and leisure equipment to a field or car park and minibuses for trips and residential activities. The vehicle is used to support the work rather than becoming the focus of it.

Street-based is not detached youth work

Street-based youth work takes place exclusively on the street. By contrast, detached youth work can happen wherever young people may be found. Detached youth workers might work in libraries, cafés, shopping centres and people's homes etc., as well as on the street. The inclusion of other places extends its reach and reflects the realities of young people's lives. Few, if any, young people spend all their time on the street. These other places are, unlike schools and colleges, essentially non-formal environments where young people are not obliged to engage in particular activities. Most might be described as 'public settings', and it is in these that most detached youth work contacts are made. They can encompass public spaces, such as parks and cemeteries etc. in addition to 'streets'.

A historical analysis of detached youth work

The origins of detached youth work lie in sociological studies of teenage gangs and subsequent street work aimed at diverting or rehabilitating them from delinquency. There was an emphasis on the potential of this work to engage young people seen as 'hard-to-reach' or 'unclubbable'. Over time, this work increasingly embraced educational perspectives and action research (thereby supporting a clearer understanding of the issues and concerns to be addressed and the methodologies to support this).

The Albermarle Report (1960, para 186) provided a further impetus, suggesting *"Peripatetic youth workers, not attached directly to any organisation or premises, who would work with existing groups or gangs of young people ... Only by going out to them shall we discover how to gain their confidence, to meet their needs and to make them aware of more genuinely rewarding pursuits."*

Over the next two decades, detached youth work shifted from being experimental to permanent and part of mainstream provision. It also addressed race and gender imbalances.

During the 1980s and 1990s, funding and social policy imperatives resulted in a shift back to those young people disinclined to engage with the wider youth service. This led many other non youth-work agencies to adopt detached and outreach approaches. Existing detached youth workers became co-opted into the drive to re-engage young people not in education, employment or training (NEET) (not least through the wider *Connexions* strategy). Detached youth workers were thus expected to contribute to a range of other agendas such as truancy, teenage pregnancy, sexual health, drugs, and Community Safety. While this shift recognised the need to work flexibly with young people, many programmes became increasingly prescribed. They were criticised for not appreciating the complexity of many young people's lives and the subtleties of effective detached youth work practice.

For a fuller account and related bibliography see Bernard Davies (2001) and Appendix 1.

Towards an authentic definition

An authentic definition of detached youth work thus emerges. This is consistent with previous research commissioned by the Joseph Rowntree Foundation:

Detached work endeavours to provide a broad-based, open-ended, social education in which the problems and issues to be dealt with, and the manner in which they are dealt with, emerges from dialogue between the young person and the youth worker.

Crimmens et al., 2004:14

This definition illustrates that, compared to other forms of youth work, detached youth work is less institutional. It focuses on engaging young people who are not accessing services, particularly when barriers exist to their participation. The significance of an authentic definition becomes apparent; it shapes responses to the question: "Why do we need detached youth work at all?" Asking *who* detached youth workers work with helps answer this question. The answer to this is intrinsic to defining detached youth work. This is explored further in *Who should detached youth workers be working with?*, see below.

The aims of detached youth work

The aims of detached youth work are thus informed by this definition. They are clearly illustrated in the work of (Burgess & Burgess, 2006:74):

- *to make contact and be available to young people in the settings of their choosing;*
- *to work with young people through programmes of personal and social education, which help them gain knowledge and recognise new opportunities in the world around them;*
- *to build effective and meaningful relationships with young people through regular contact, mutual trust, respect and understanding;*
- *to identify and respond to the needs and agendas of individuals and groups of young people by developing appropriate strategies for action which are both educational and fun;*
- *to support and challenge young people's attitudes and actions towards issues such as: unemployment, drugs, alcohol, poverty, racism, sexism, disability, housing, health, sexuality, criminality, peer, parental and community pressure;*

- *to enable young people to take more control over their lives and create experiences with them which enable them to make informed choices;*
- *to support appropriate action that young people take resulting from their own ideas and suggestions;*
- *to work within the framework of equal opportunities;*
- *to bridge the gaps in understanding between the local community and young people;*
- *to highlight issues affecting young people and act as advocates for and with them within the wider community and world.*

Guideline:
- **All agencies need a clear statement of aims. This should inform objectives and anticipated outcomes. All staff need to be familiar with this material so that it can guide both their professional development and the identity of the project.**

FINDINGS & ANALYSIS

The identity of detached youth work

The issue of the identity of detached youth work is central to the research findings.

The views of respondents

In many of the projects, there is no coherent definition of detached youth work. Working definitions rarely match the authentic definition reached here. Some answer the question: 'What is detached youth work?' by saying that it is a response to a variety of youth-oriented problems in the local community. Others give more sophisticated interpretations that focused on its educative dimensions.

The study reveals that many longer-serving detached youth workers and managers believe that definitions of detached youth work have become 'fudged' in recent years. They argue that there is a profound difference between what detached youth work was in the past and what it is has become today. They see detached youth work as 'losing its way'.

Detached youth work manager: *"These days there are several different mutations of what detached youth work is."*

Detached youth work manager: *"The concept of what detached youth work is has become fudged."*

Manager: *"Detached youth work is losing its educational focus."*

Evidence for this shift in emphasis is not just anecdotal. A thorough analysis of historical accounts of detached youth work (see Appendix 1) and, indeed, more recent accounts such as *Don't Shoot: I'm a Detached Youth Worker* (Burgess and Burgess, 2006) which describes the life of a project over many years, reveal the increased impact of external **demands** on detached youth work. This trend translates into a reduction in professional autonomy within the process of planning detached youth work. In tandem, there has been a marked shift away from the previous centrality of young people's issues and needs, as identified by them.

Detached youth work is now expected to encompass a wide range of social interventions, many of which detached youth workers themselves don't recognise. In short, it has become a 'catch all' description for a range of ways of working with young people. Many of these methods have their own distinctive characteristics, which differ significantly from the authentic definition of detached youth work identified above. Specifically, there is significant concern about the identification of detached youth work as, principally, a mechanism for dealing with anti-social behaviour:

Detached youth worker: *"I'm not a troubleshooter. We need to fight a battle against 'hot spotting': we're not the fourth emergency service."*

There is an almost unanimous desire to 'reclaim' detached youth work as a distinctive form of youth work practice:

Manager: *"We need some disciples to restate what detached youth work is."*

The desire to refocus on the needs of young people is most apparent:

Detached youth worker: *"I am here for young people; the work should not be informed by the needs of others."*

Observations of practice

Posing the question: 'What is detached youth work?" is one thing; observing practice is another. This research included accompanying several detached youth workers, in each of the areas visited, in their work.

Examples of detached youth work visited include:

- Street-work, usually conducted by a small team of workers in several areas in the same evening. Often, this means driving significant distances between areas and having to fill out monitoring forms in the car because it is considered too far and too time-consuming to go back to 'base'.
- Sexual health outreach work in various public spaces, including on the street, in parks and outside shops (apparently a popular meeting place for young people). The sites are visited by workers in a minibus. The minibus is seen as necessary because the venues are far apart, but also because it provides an independent space for talking to young people and distributing condoms (though the bus offers no privacy from onlookers).
- Building-based low-intervention youth clubs. The detached youth workers, in essence, act as key-holders for a sports pavilion in a village, thereby facilitating access to an apparently much needed social space for young people to gather.
- Structured group work (planning a campaign) in a room within a community centre. Again, access to the space has been negotiated by the youth workers.
- Mobile provision. Providing, essentially, a mobile low-intervention space for young people to meet in a village (although there was a village hall nearby where "the young people are not allowed to go." (sic.)).
- 'Hot spot' and 'reassurance ward' responses. Working with young people in areas that have been identified by other agencies (e.g. Community Safety partnerships) on the basis of youth nuisance.
- Specific time-limited projects, e.g. 'a crime project' where there was a prescribed calendar of activities for young people, including talks by criminal justice personnel.

The findings from these observations of practice are revealing. It is clear that generic 'street-based' detached youth, where workers have a base in, and walk around, a local 'patch', is very rare. Instead, detached youth workers undertake a range of activities in disparate environments. Many of these activities appear to have little to do with the authentic definition of detached youth work reached above. This finding presents a clear challenge to all agencies. They must reach a consensus on what detached youth work is and they must then provide the **support** and **training** so that all staff can confidently articulate this to all stakeholders. Detached youth workers and their managers cannot expect colleagues in partner agencies always to know, understand and, therefore, sympathise with or appreciate the detail of their work. That is to say, those partners, without knowing what detached youth work is and does, cannot themselves advocate on behalf of detached youth work.

Guideline:
- **Agencies must develop a wider understanding of what detached youth work is and the contribution it can make. They must take a proactive and robust stance, using the 'authentic' definition outlined here to do so. A coherent definition of detached youth work is essential for this. The process should include distinguishing between detached youth work and the generic concept of detached work. Equally, the question: "*Is* this detached youth work?" is vital so as to 'define out' practice that does not meet this definition. This step must not be skipped: reflecting on definitions is important and has implications for the training (see also separate section) of all those involved in detached youth work.**

Related analysis

This shift in emphasis is the result of local and national pressures. These mostly come in the form of demands imposed by funders and the range of social policy agendas to which detached youth work is now expected to contribute.

Many detached youth workers are concerned that their practice has become **reactive** (and often in a 'knee-jerk' way). They also express concern that detached youth work now exists as a default option for intervening into a wide range of social problems (both perceived and actual). This trend, they argue, is exacerbated by partner agencies and, indeed, some managers of detached youth work asking: "What can detached work do here?", rather than a more enlightened: "What is the appropriate response in this situation?"

Almost all detached youth work now occurs in the context of 'partnership work'. Where detached youth workers and their managers assert a strong sense of 'what detached youth work is', partner agencies have developed their knowledge and understanding accordingly. But where this does not occur, the **demands** fed down from partnerships [typically through the dominant power players within these partnerships] result in detached youth work allowing itself to be sucked into a range of other (different) forms of intervention. Examples include 'rapid response' units and projects with specific issue-based agendas.

One detached youth worker recounts how he was so exasperated at being asked to do things that he believed had little or nothing to do with detached youth work that he lost his temper in a partnership meeting. Ironically, this led to a request for him to detail exactly what his job was. The worker had to "dig down deep" for answers. By doing so, though, he was able to promote a much deeper understanding of detached youth work among those present who, he acknowledged, could not be expected to know. Thereafter, his relationship with partner agencies was much more productive, with an emphasis on how detached youth work could, with *its* frame of reference, add value to the work of others.

Detached youth worker: *"I am not here for this; I am here for the young people."*

Many of those involved in detached youth work call for a more enlightened *responsiveness*, in which intervention is more considered and based on reflection and analysis. In any given situation, managers and partners should first ask themselves: *"Is detached youth work an appropriate response?"* This approach should help them stick to detached youth work's primary commitment, which is to young people's education and welfare rather than to alleviating social problems seen to be caused by young people.

Senior detached youth worker: *"It's important for me to say what I do. I don't want to be measured against anti-social behaviour targets."*

Detached youth worker: *"The way I am being asked to work means I don't feel like I am a detached youth worker any more. I see detached youth work as 'pro-actionary'. That's what makes it different from the work of most other agencies; they are reactionary and want to stop young people being young. They see young people negatively and as problems; detached youth work sees them positively."*

Detached youth worker: *"We need to work as closely as possible to a strong model of what detached youth work is."*

For many, this emphasis on problems 'caused by' young people instead of problems facing young people skews the essential nature of the detached youth work process. It shifts the focus of detached youth work from young people's identification of their needs to one in which their needs (and the responses to them) are determined and prescribed by adults. This translates into a demand to **'deliver'** a range of **'outcomes'**. This model disregards the value and importance of an open-ended process upon which effective detached youth work has historically been based.

There are also concerns that detached youth work training regimes and, as a result, workers' professional development, now reflect this change in focus. Some of those interviewed suggest that a new generation of detached youth workers is emerging: those that lack the knowledge (of theory and history), skills and attitudes necessary to work effectively on the streets.

Some go further and argue that this shift in emphasis now routinely shapes a version of detached youth work that bears no resemblance to its historical and value-based roots. Most significantly, there is the suggestion that this has led to a focus on young people who are more easily recruited into outcomes-oriented programmes. Detached youth work's historical constituency is precisely the opposite, comprising those young people who suffer most from social exclusion. What an irony this reveals: while social policy increasingly wants and tries to make contact and work with those socially excluded, the mechanisms put in place to achieve this appear to be counterproductive. Not only do they exacerbate the exclusion of these young people, but they also deprive them of one of the few methods of working that supports their inclusion.

Detached youth workers are also concerned that the work of other agencies masquerades as youth work and this affects how others perceive *their* work. For example, detached youth workers tell of street wardens taking groups of young people ten-pin bowling. This activity had received a lot of publicity and had been claimed as 'a great piece of youth work'. For detached youth workers, however, this activity was entirely leisure-oriented and failed to involve young people in planning, design and evaluation (seen as the educational dimensions of youth work rather than leisure provision). Some see these activities as undermining detached youth work. There is also some hostility to the high level of resources invested in these other initiatives (see also **Funding**).

There is concern among many of those interviewed that other agencies are 'piggy-backing' good detached youth work. Many conclude that they had to be able to demonstrate what it was about their work that adds further value to more leisure-oriented work provision. Without this, many workers fear that these other agencies would be "ready and waiting to step in and pick up youth work contracts" even though, as some argue, they are not actually doing youth work.

Detached youth worker: *"If we are too precious about what we do and what we don't do, other agencies will step in."*

Educating the commissioners of services is also therefore important.

This point alone illustrates the need for a clear description of what sets detached youth work apart from others who work with young people. This is all the more urgent because many detached youth workers (and indeed managers) themselves have only a limited understanding of this. This lack of awareness is particularly prevalent among poorly trained part-time workers and managers who have little or no experience of the practice of detached youth work.

Guidelines:
- **Those involved in detached youth work must be able to assert a strong and confident vision of what detached youth work is. In particular, they must be able to articulate its educational focus and role in engaging young people who are not accessing services. Without this, they are at risk of being co-opted (either unwittingly or by the manipulation of others) into activities that contradict their aims and values and meet the needs not of young people but of others. They must develop and stick to a coherent and authentic definition of what detached youth work is. Detached youth workers need to be able to say, with confidence: "This is what I do."**

> Clearly, this has implications not only for good practice, but also for training regimes (see also Training).
>
> - Conversely, managers must not be bull-headed about what detached youth work is not. This may lead to a situation where real opportunities for positive interventions are ruled out. What is needed is a considered approach to determining whether detached youth work *is* an appropriate response, and what form an intervention should take. There may, of course, be times when tensions occur between the demands and drivers (see also separate section) experienced by detached youth workers and a commitment to authentic detached youth work. Many of these can be avoided by the earlier preparation of job descriptions that are true to this definition. Without this to back them up, detached youth workers who seek to resist demands on them to act in, for them, ways that contradict with a value-based stance, risk breach of contract. Ultimately, excellence in detached youth work may require workers to say, "no, this is not my job". To do so, though, they will need the support not only of a sound job description, authentic definition and relevant training, but also the full backing of their managers. A dialogue between workers and managers is, therefore, essential.

Why do detached youth work? Moving away from detached youth work as a default option

The research found that the rationale behind decisions about why detached youth work should be undertaken was varied and often complex.

In some places, detached youth work takes places specifically because there is no other form of youth service. In one area, local youth centres have been closed as they were seen to pose health and safety risks and no funding for repairs could be found. In an effort to maintain some level of service provision in that area, particularly to the young people who had previously attended the club, the centre-based workers are re-deployed in a detached capacity.

Elsewhere, decisions to deploy detached youth workers are strongly influenced by a wide range of external demands, i.e. detached youth work is appropriated by other agendas and thus loses its identity and value. Typically, service managers report pressure to respond to a range of issues and problems (most often within the context of Community Safety). The irony is that this process may ultimately lead to the disappearance of detached youth work (as defined above) altogether.

Detached youth work often takes place regardless of whether it is the most appropriate response to identified issues and problems. For example, some workers were working with young people who regularly attend youth clubs. In an attempt to get some 'quick wins' and establish relationships with young people early on in the project's life, the workers decided that the quickest way to get themselves known was to contact young people who were existing members of centre-based youth clubs. This led to them working with these same young people on days when the youth club was closed. No thought is given to increasing youth club capacity to meet need, to providing a service to young people who were not already accessing the centre, to the significance and importance of detached youth workers' independence from the centre or to managed **'fit'** (see elsewhere) between different sections of the youth service.

> **Guidelines:**
> - **Detached youth work managers, particularly when working in partnership settings, may need to argue (forcefully if necessary) for a more considered examination of what is the most appropriate response to a particular issue. An objective analysis (particularly one that tries to do justice to the values implicit in an authentic definition of detached youth work) would conclude that detached youth work is not automatically what is needed. This position is in sharp contrast to that implied (currently) by the seemingly ever-present question: "What can detached youth work do here?" – which clearly assumes that detached youth work *is* an appropriate response to *all* situations. Those involved in detached youth work must step back and ask: "*Is* detached youth work what is needed here?"**
>
> - **Taking this stance relies on the implementation of a wider strategy to help those involved in detached youth work and others from partner agencies learn about detached youth work. Essential planning questions might include: "*Why* do you think detached youth work is an appropriate response?" and "Who *are* the best people to intervene in this situation?" Ultimately, the development of excellent practice relies on promoting a cultural position that is *not* based on the immediate reaction that problems associated with young people automatically call for detached youth work to 'solve them'. Indeed it is essential for those currently experiencing this scenario to move beyond this damaging 'default mentality' if practice is to be excellent. A strategic response to these issues should include efforts to agree protocols with partner agencies for detached youth worker involvement. These protocols must take account of rationale behind the work, anticipated outcomes, resources needed, duration of intervention, confidentiality etc.**
>
> - **Doing this will reveal the importance of a clear delineation between detached youth work and other forms of work with young people. Detached youth work, it should be argued, is a mechanism for working with young people who are not accessing other forms of service provision. Where no other provision exists, detached youth work should only be employed as a temporary measure until action can be taken to meet the needs of young people for whom centre-based or other provision is most appropriate.**
>
> - **The role of management then, effectively, is to scrutinise and respond to the (many) demands that impact on detached youth work. This includes exploring what and in whose interests these drivers act. The relative importance of each has to be discussed. The interests of adults are not necessarily the same as those of young people. Decisions about where to deploy detached youth work resources must prioritise the needs of young people – to do otherwise is quite simply not detached youth work. Where this assessment reveals that detached youth workers could play a positive role (i.e. creating benefit for young people), decisions still need to be made about what <u>level</u> of service is needed in order to ensure interventions are effective. This**

> level of service must be informed qualitatively, i.e. be consistent with providing a quality service. Where resources are limited, managers have a responsibility to state what level of <u>quality</u> (effective) service is possible within the proposed resource allocation. This might mean, for example, working in fewer areas than others would like.
>
> Standard:
> - This research considers the minimum staffing resource for achieving excellence to be one full-time professionally trained detached youth worker and two locally trained part-timers, each working a minimum of three sessions a week. Ideally this level of resource should be deployed in all local areas identified as having substantive need (see *Community Profiling* for a wider discussion as to how these areas are identified). This supports *Findings* of the Joseph Rowntree Foundation (2004).

Where do detached youth workers work? The importance of assessing need

Where detached youth workers work is a complex issue. A range of demands and local issues have an impact on this.

None of the managers interviewed feel they have total control over where their detached youth workers worked. While many indicate having significant autonomy, others feel decisions about where staff worked are largely out of their hands. These responses appear to parallel funding arrangements, with managers of mainstream-funded projects having the greatest autonomy. Conversely, where detached youth work was funded by particular, thematic, partnership arrangements, managers often report great pressure to deploy resources in certain areas. This pressure often comes from councillors and others within 'partnership frameworks'. It is most often based on a desire to see certain problems addressed in specific areas. Often these are associated with incidences of antisocial behaviour.

Detached youth worker: *"We get told to work in certain areas because they have been identified as 'reassurance wards' [areas where the local crime and disorder partnership wants to make an impact on antisocial behaviour and perceptions about community safety]."*

Where detached youth work is intrinsic to local partnerships arrangements (and this is almost everywhere), these partners appear to exert ever-increasing pressure not only on where detached youth workers work, but also on many other decisions associated with practice. This often includes the use of detached youth work to pursue a variety of social policy agendas.

Some youth services, acutely aware of these demands, try to adopt a strategic and pragmatic response to these demands. They, though, are only too aware of the ethical dilemmas associated with this approach:

Detached youth work manager: *"It might make political sense to work in a particular area for a while [even though that might not be where we'd want to work]. Being seen to be doing something in that area might give us the political capital we need to secure extra resources and funding in the longer term."*

It is clear that a range of demands shape deployment decisions. The perceived needs of young people rarely feature as the main consideration. Often the service's own (bureaucratic) needs, and those of partnership structures, elected officials, funders and community associations, as expressed though Community Safety mechanisms, hold greater sway.

This situation is further complicated by the sheer *quantity* of demands. In attempting to respond to the many rather than the few, detached youth work resources are inevitably spread thinly. Most managers express concern about the impact this has on the *quality* of practice, but are resigned to the limits of their authority. This can lead to only limited scrutiny of the implications of these decisions. Typically, individual detached youth workers are often tasked to work in several areas in a given week. This has a two-fold effect. First, it compromises their ability to get to know communities that are often disparate and diverse, at an intimate level. Second, it limits their contact with young people. Indeed, none of the detached youth workers interviewed were doing more than two sessions a week with any given group of young people.

Most of the detached youth workers interviewed work in at least two different areas each week. Some work in several areas, and a few focus on a single area. As a result, rarely do detached youth workers have an in-depth knowledge of the community and area in which they work. Limited contact also compromises their capacity to develop in-depth relationships with young people *and* the wider community. And it restricts opportunities to engage with community involvement structures, such as area panels and forums. This reduces their ability to advocate on behalf of young people and undertake community development activities, such as making contact with potential supporters and local agencies to which they might refer young people.

The study also finds that, in some cases, detached youth workers are deployed to cover absences of centre-based colleagues. This reveals that some managers may perceive centre-based activities as being of higher status and, therefore, deserving priority. Most often, this seems to be a product of a 'visibility' imperative, whereby an open youth centre is seen to have a significantly greater political resonance than detached youth work.

> **Guidelines:**
> - Needs assessment is an essential element of a systematic approach to deciding where detached youth work takes place. Excellence demands this. It should draw upon evidence such as indices of multiple deprivation and local reporting from agencies working with young people. Reports of youth nuisance, for example, do not constitute sufficient evidence on their own of the need for a detached youth work intervention. Where there is pressure (political or otherwise) to work in certain areas, these demands must be subject to similar scrutiny. For excellent detached youth work to occur, young people's needs should take precedence over those of other stakeholders. Where necessary, managers must assert that their [a detached youth work] analysis carries the most weight. Ultimately, detached youth workers and their managers should be the chief arbiters of where the work takes place.
> - The practice of 'robbing Peter to pay Paul', whereby the resourcing of centre-based activities takes precedence over that of detached youth work, damages the quality of detached youth work. It should be avoided by all who wish to provide excellent detached youth work. Wherever possible, the funding and staffing of detached youth work should be independent.
> - Ideally, detached youth workers should concentrate their efforts in a single, specific, spatially defined, community. They should have the capacity to invest significant levels of time with key groups of young people (over and above the one or two sessions needed to maintain contact with them). By working in one area (rather than many) there is more opportunity to do developmental work with young people, the wider community and service–provider networks.

Community profiling

Community profiling is the process of developing an intimate knowledge of a local community.

The study found very little evidence of in-depth community profiling. Some of those interviewed view this as being of limited relevance, since decisions about where to work are made elsewhere (outside of the project and within partnership settings). Community profiling activities are (where they did take place) often secondary to partnership-focused assessment regimes that tend to focus on problems that needed to be solved. See: '*Where* **do detached youth workers work?**', above for a fuller analysis.

The lack of in-depth community profiling appears to limit the extent to which detached youth work projects can become embedded in the community. The corollary of not knowing local people is, of course, that *they* do not know the detached youth workers. This undermines the potential for that community to contribute to the detached youth work project. The project may miss out, for example, on information, advice and insights into local culture, volunteer support, practical help and resources, and broadening the base of the work in support of wider community development aims. Limited contact with local adults also undermines 'promotional' work. This is a key catalyst in inspiring community involvement in the project's activities and management, a pre-requisite of local 'ownership' and a catalyst for promoting inter-generational engagement.

Guidelines:

- Excellent detached youth work invariably takes place in the context of a spatially defined community. This is essential to building a broad base and rich resource of contacts, alliances, relationships and networks, without which detached youth work will be isolated and weakened. Wherever possible, detached youth workers should work in a single area, in order to develop an intimate knowledge of its people and its issues.

- Excellent detached youth work depends upon a strong understanding of the local community and all this implies. To reach this position, an in-depth community profile must be undertaken in all areas that have been identified by needs assessment processes.

- Community profiles should be comprehensive. They are particularly important when developing new projects. They should focus on the needs of young people and consider all available evidence that helps define this need (as distinct from the needs of others). Activities should include making contact with key agencies and community members, observations of where and when young people gather, and indicators of local issues (such as the prevalence of graffiti or vandalism). This process should determine whether detached youth work is an appropriate intervention and, if so, identify which groups of young people might be approached and which issues might be explored with them.

- Community profile findings should be the most important reference for practice and, in particular, where the work should takes place. Managers should attempt to recruit staff whose skills and experience reflect these findings.

- Throughout the life of the project, community profiles should be regularly up-dated. That way, detached youth workers will stay up to-date with locally changing issues and be able to respond to them. Those involved in detached youth work must, therefore, ensure that they have regular and meaningful contact with local people and with those who represent agencies and voluntary organisations.

Who should detached youth workers be working with?

Very few of the projects visited were working with young people over 16. There was a sense that the workers don't feel equipped to work with this age group (it calls for more emphasis on the subtleties of process, rather than providing leisure opportunities to those who are younger). Also, some of those interviewed suggest that related targets made it 'uneconomical' to invest their time in trying to develop relationships with an older age group. This is largely because to do so requires more time, and it is hard to identify significant numbers to meet targets. Despite this, a number of detached youth workers and their managers are adamant that what distinguishes detached youth work from the work of other agencies is its *capacity* to work with this age group and with those classified as socially excluded. Other agencies have systematically failed to engage this cohort or have even decided not to try in the first place. Consequently, where detached youth workers are not working with this age group, the chances are no other agencies are doing so either, (even though almost all social policy identified this cohort as *the* key target audience). Working with 16 to 19-year-olds is seen by some managers as "the key to evidencing the worth of detached youth work". These social policy drivers also shape national expectations that all Youth Services are in contact with the full age range of young people. Effective detached youth work clearly has an important role to play in achieving this.

Some workers say that they had cut off contact with groups who were "too challenging" or "whose behaviour was too bad". They have, instead, turned their attention to working with "the good kids, who often don't get a chance".

Targeting through genericism: going the extra mile

None of the detached youth workers interviewed were comfortable with the idea of targeting specific individuals. They see this as conflicting with their belief that young people should be entitled to determine the terms of their engagement with detached youth workers; their voluntary association is seen as a defining feature of the work. Some detached youth workers are able to offer extra support to particular individuals, but they do this on the basis of initial contact with them through the peer groups that they meet during the course of their detached youth work. They argue that young people's presence on the street is often, in itself, evidence of their social exclusion and related issues that lead them not to access services. Workers state that by engaging with them in this context, it is possible to avoid a 'case-load' approach and avoid the possibility of stigmatising young people. In getting to know young people and developing relationships with them, workers describe how some young people present a range of problems for which detached youth workers could then offer support. These young people are not necessarily those seen as socially excluded by external determinants.

Detached youth worker: *"Some of the young people are really challenging; but the point is that by going the extra mile with those individuals it is possible to work successfully with them."*

Many detached youth workers acknowledge the potential of their practice to help alleviate social exclusion, and that detached youth work has a long history of working with those who are social excluded (Arnold et al.,1989). They are, though, concerned that it is increasingly difficult to maintain a flexible and open-ended orientation to their work. The lack of these characteristics, they say, compromises their ability to work with those whose need is greatest.

Guidelines:
- **As we have seen, one of the primary functions of a community profile is to identify groups of young people with whom it may be appropriate to work. Where the profiling step is missed out, there is often a tendency to make contact and work with the first group that comes along. This should be avoided. Instead, decisions about whom detached youth workers should attempt to contact should be the result of an assessment of the diversity of groups that exists, the range of issues they present and the resources available. The desire to target a particular individual or individuals should not be part of this process. Success in engaging young people is not a foregone conclusion; young people themselves must wish to commit to these**

relationships. Their voluntary association or, indeed, disassociation, should be respected.

- Detached youth workers should undertake a constant 'access audit' of their practice. In this, they reflect on whom they are working with. Race and diversity issues and a commitment to equal opportunities should inform this analysis. They should consider whether it might be appropriate to refer young people to other forms of youth service provision. Typically, many young people's needs focus on their interest in having somewhere to go. These needs are likely better to be met by going to a youth centre. Detached youth workers should aim to facilitate this involvement. They thus maintain *their* focus on working with young people who, for more complex reasons, have needs that can be addressed only in a detached context.

- This situation is, of course, complicated where no other forms of youth provision exist. In these cases, detached youth workers face difficult questions as to who they should work with. In these circumstances, critical reflection and reviewing are important tools for decision-making. Detached youth workers should remember that working with young people who could easily be integrated into mainstream youth opportunities is tantamount to mis-using resources. And it may deprive some young people of one of the few forms of engagement that meet their needs.

Contact making / The significance of street-based contact

The study finds that detached youth workers inhabit a range of environments. Many actively make contact and work with young people in street-based settings, car parks, fields and parkland and publicly accessible buildings such as supermarkets and cafés etc. Others are often found working in more formal environments such as schools and training centres. The latter say that it is useful for making contact with young people, who would, then, recognise them when they were working on the street. The workers appear not to have considered that they might then prioritise contact with those in school rather with than those who are excluded. Likewise, there was no analysis of a potentially detrimental alliance with the school, which, as above, might put some young people off (typically those disaffected from school) engaging with them. Detached youth workers need to be seen to be independent to avoid this.

Guideline:

- Detached youth workers should be mindful of the significance of *where* they make contact with young people, as this can greatly affect *who* they work with. Meeting young people in formal environments is not usually conducive to developing relationships with those disaffected from those very institutions. The study finds that the street-based environment (in its widest sense, as described above) is the one that most readily lends itself to contacting a diverse range of young people, especially those who are socially excluded.

The importance of relationships

The importance of relationships in effective detached youth work cannot be understated. But initiating, developing and maintaining positive relationships, especially with often challenging young people, does not come easily. Many of those interviewed identify relationship-building skills as central to excellent detached youth work. Typical comments include:

Detached youth work manager (talking about one of his detached youth workers): *"I've never known anyone with that [high] level of ability to 'get alongside' so many different kinds of young people."*

But what is it to 'get alongside'? Invariably, the detached youth workers who can have communication skills of the highest order. They are adept at and committed to listening. They transmit a sense of respect for those they work with. They are patient and unassuming. The young people, in turn, respect them, leading to the growth of mutual trust. This trust is particularly important where young people do not trust others, for example 'officials' and others in authority. The young people may be highly reticent about engaging with strangers and even adults *per se*. In these circumstances, detached youth workers appreciate that they may be one of few (if not the only) positive adult role models in the life of those young people. And they commit to the responsibility that this entails. Detached youth workers report that the behaviour of young people illustrates an awareness of this: they look to the worker to set them a good example. Meeting this expectation is key to the detached youth worker being an agent of moral education and true to a value base that is epitomised by respect and trust.

Many detached youth workers are aware of the sensitivities associated with these relationships. They argue that relationships have to be given time to develop, and that being too demanding in the earlier stages of contact can be counter-productive:

Detached youth worker: *"You have to hang out to hang in."*

This study finds that a number of workers exhibit these higher order communication skills and that they are able to use them to make contact, engage, and develop relationships with young people. Largely, this occurs where managers appreciate that doing this well takes time. Other workers express frustration about pressures to 'move the work on'. In some cases, detached workers talk of being given a specified time to identify a group and undertake a programme.

There are other important temporal aspects to the theme of relationships. While many young people will engage with detached youth workers on a regular basis, others 'dip in' and 'dip out'. This often happens with older young people who have previously had high levels of contact. But relationships appear to live on. This is especially important where young people experience problems as they get older. One detached youth worker recounts how a young man contacted him some two years after their last meeting to ask for support at a particularly difficult time in his life. This illustrates the value of detached youth workers with a long-term presence in a particular community. It also shows how young people do not simply move out of social exclusion and remain thereafter 'included'. This is confirmed in the findings of the Social Exclusion Unit (2005). The life courses of many young people, as with many adults, can be marked by negative experiences, such as bereavement or problems with family or school. These events can lead to them moving in and out of social exclusion. A number of detached youth workers who do have such long-term contacts describe how these young people have re-engaged with them at these times precisely because of their trust in and access to the workers.

> **Guideline:**
> - **An ability to communicate is the bedrock of good practice. Success almost always depends upon being able to 'get alongside' young people and develop relationships with them. Where good communication is absent, meaningful and effective interventions are impossible. Detached youth workers must be given time to invest in these relationships. For some groups of young people this takes time. Demands for measurable and swift progress can undermine attempts to develop relationships. These demands often focus on the [potential] product of interventions without regard for the process necessary to achieve outcomes. They must be resisted if the work is to be effective. Managers must take this into account, particularly when responding to the demands of funders whose (often limited) knowledge of process-oriented ways of working (see below) often expresses itself as unrealistic timescales for achieving outcomes. Wherever possible, services should commit to enduring and longer-term programmes of intervention. These are much more likely to be successful. They symbolise a long-term investment in a community.**

Process or programme? Detached youth workers or detached teachers?

This study raises particular concerns about a growing emphasis on pre-scribed activities and programmes. These are in contrast to process-oriented ways of working, in which the needs and interests of young people, as revealed in dialogue with workers, guide the work.

Pressure comes from the wider social policy agenda, via partner agencies and funders keen to see certain outcomes. Perhaps they can be forgiven for taking this stance, as there appear to be few attempts by those involved in detached youth work to promote the importance of process-oriented methods. Most worryingly, many detached youth workers appear to have limited or no knowledge or experience of these methods themselves. This is most prevalent among new and part-time detached youth workers, many of whom have had little or no training in the theory and practice of process-oriented methodology. As a consequence, a great deal of practice now concentrates on the delivery of pre-determined programmes. Contemporary practice appears increasingly devoid of the characteristics that define it as authentic detached youth work, (see above). In many respects, there appears to have been a profound shift: away from the facilitation of <u>learning</u> and towards <u>teaching</u> about issues (many of which have not been identified through discussions with young people).

The only attempts to resist this shift mostly come from senior detached youth workers. These lone voices believe their work is now radically different from past years and that these pressures have compromised their ability to develop relationships with those young people most socially excluded. Some workers argue that, without negotiation, it is indeed impossible to engage these young people, many of whom have had a negative experience of formal learning.

Across the agencies visited, there appears little or no strategic attempt formally to train part-time workers in process-oriented methods. Neither is there evidence of attempts to facilitate their learning through creating opportunities to observe the work of, and be mentored by, more experienced and skilled practitioners, many of whom have learnt these skills as part of their professional training. Many of these skills and dispositions are therefore not being passed on. Where professionally qualified workers are also subject to pressure to deliver prescribed programmes, this clearly disregards and undermines the values that underpin their training, which many chose to undertake because of a desire to work democratically.

This shift away from young people's **participation** (see below) is ironic given its significance in social policy. It manifests itself in one clear way. Workers initiate conversations on themes that are determined *without* as opposed to *within* their relationships with young people. Often these themes reflect the interests of funders and are linked to specific desired outcomes. There is only limited evidence of detached youth workers listening to and building upon the conversations of young people. Indeed the study witnessed few attempts by detached youth workers to begin with day-to-day conversations and to identify issues emerging from an *agenda-free* dialogue.

The study witnessed several examples of specific issue-based programmes being set up by workers. Conversations often focused on trying to recruit young people on to these programmes. In this sense, a great deal of practice exhibited the characteristics of project and outreach work, if not teaching. This is far removed from the authentic definition of detached youth work identified above.

Typical observation of practice: Detached youth worker/s: *"We've got a health/crime project; do you want to take part?"*

This is not to say that detached youth work has no history of working with issues. On the contrary. Historical accounts are full of issue-based work. These issues, though, largely emerged from a dialogue between the young people and the workers. That rarely happens these days.

Many of these programmes do succeed in recruiting some young people. But the motivation of many of these young people appears to focus on simply wanting to do something with friends and was not subject to in-depth scrutiny. Other young people appear, by contrast, uncomfortable with this model and tend to distance themselves from the workers and these opportunities:

Observation of practice: *Attempts to encourage young people to fill in a record of progress were met enthusiastically by some young people, but appeared to act as a barrier with others such that the young people moved away.*

In this scenario, a booklet was used to record young people's 'achievements' for which they could earn prizes. While some young people appeared to be happy to work through the booklet, others noticeably shunned it. The workers focused on the former.

The study found many instances of this 'pistachio effect'. As with eating the shelled nuts, the easiest to handle get picked first, while the 'tougher nuts' are dealt with later, or discarded altogether. In detached youth work, this means that many workers (often unwittingly) focus their attention on young people who are more easily engaged or less challenging to work with:

Detached youth worker (in response to question about why they were working with a particular group): *"They're easier to work with; the previous group's behaviour was bad and we couldn't trust them."*

Detached youth worker: *"There is a tendency to drop them"* [those who are challenging and difficult to work with].

There is therefore evidence of detached youth workers increasingly targeting young people they judge will be interested in taking part in these programmes. Young people who already experience social exclusion may, as a result, be excluded even more.

Some detached youth workers appreciate that while many young people are keen to join in accredited programmes, others "won't go near them". These workers know that other strategies are needed:

Detached youth worker: "The numbers game gets problematic, we need a diverse tool box; what works with some doesn't work with others".

Other workers, on the other hand, seem oblivious. They have not considered that a focus on prescribed outcomes and accreditation might act as a barrier to working with some young people.

Many detached youth workers crave support to develop their [these] personal 'tool kits'. Others fail to appreciate that different ways of working are important for equality of opportunity. Managerial influences in this regard are also significant. Some managers are reluctant or unable to underwrite the time and resource implications of **training.** Equally, some managers also appear to lack an appreciation of the importance of multi-pronged intervention strategies. They expect often poorly trained detached youth workers to be able to engage successfully with any and all young people.

These processes illustrate a shift away from conversation-oriented youth work. The work increasingly bypasses its historical constituency of young people who, for a variety of complex reasons, are challenging, rarely access services, often have a history of underachievement and are disaffected from formal learning.

Some workers are concerned that the use of mass-produced 'achievement ranking systems' and associated 'rewards schemes' is driven by an obsession with qualifications and a desire to compensate for poor outcomes elsewhere:

Detached youth work manager: *"I really don't think that benchmarked targets are appropriate to detached youth work. I think we have been handed these targets because of the failing of secondary education."*

Historically, young people, in conversation with detached youth workers, learnt to articulate their interests and concerns and were supported in designing, building and delivering activities and programmes that met these needs. These days though, this research reveals that young people are rarely challenged to identify issues that are of interest and concern to *them* or helped to develop mechanisms to address these issues *through their own actions*. Rather, they are offered a diet of consumer options from which to choose. This undermines a central tenet of youth work: supporting young people in becoming initiators, creators and developers of curriculum [what they learn], shaped by critical dialogue with detached youth workers.

This emphasis on the 'pre-scription' and 'pre-design' of programmes shifts the emphasis of the work from young people's **participation** to young people's **consumption**, and from youth work to teaching.

Some detached youth workers make valiant attempts to square this circle. Typically, where offers of funding are made to deliver a specified agenda, the workers take a pragmatic view of the dilemma they face. They try to be true to process *and* work to increase benefit for young people. While they are adamant that their work should not be about *doing to* young people (i.e. recruiting them for specific programmes), they seek to link up these agendas with groups of young people whose needs and interests they already know *on the basis of* existing and established relationships. Actively going out to recruit a new group for a prescribed programme is, however, a step too far, they say.

In conclusion, youth services' and funders' needs conflict with a young person-led approach to detached youth work. This acts as a barrier to excellence. Instead of engaging young people in a dialogue about programme design, the tendency is for a worker-led "let's do this …" approach. Ultimately, this affects young people's experience of detached youth work; 'pre-scription' 'filters down to young people' such that that their agency (involvement in the process) extends to no more that opting in or opting out, depending on how they feel. They become used to simply choosing from the options available to them, instead of creating those options themselves. This, then, becomes their view of what detached youth work is and does.

Guideline:
- **Excellent detached youth work is, as has been seen already, a form of democratic practice. All those involved in its development must commit to using models of practice that offer and challenge young people to work out how they can be involved. Young people need to be encouraged to take responsibility for programme design and, wherever possible, for its implementation. If these elements are missing, claims that young people's participation is valued ring hollow.**

Standard:

- The participatory credentials of detached youth work must regularly and consistently be assessed. Pre-scripted programmes should be avoided.

Reflection, Reviewing and Analysis: The centrality of good judgement-making

None of the detached youth workers contacted through this study receive **non-managerial supervision**. Few are engaged in any systematic reflection and reviewing of their practice. Where this does occur it is rarely overseen by an experienced senior worker who might be able to facilitate a critical analysis of the work. Usually, those who have worked together will, after a session, write a brief account of what happened and make a note of monitoring information. There is little to suggest that detached youth workers analyse this information later. Recordings and monitoring forms are rarely used to inform future practice. Often collecting material as recorded outcomes appears to be done as an end itself. Not once did a worker refer to how the recording of outcomes has influenced practice or contributed substantively to the assessment of young people's learning. The study concludes that reflection on practice is often weak. This hinders workers' ability to 'reflect-in-action'.

The study finds few examples of workers exhibiting higher order analytical skills. This is especially true among part-time workers who have had limited professional training.

All interviewees welcomed the chance to discuss their work in a consistent and systemic way. Many confess that they never do so normally:

Detached youth worker: *"It's been great to have this opportunity to really think and talk about what I am doing. We never usually do this."*

Detached youth worker: *"This is the first occasion where I have taken time to really think about and explore exactly what detached youth work is."*

Note: These comments are typical also of many made by managers.

Guidelines:

- **Managers should make sure that they and detached youth workers have enough time and support to analyse both the theory and practice of detached youth work and their role in it. Excellent detached youth work relies on a constant commitment to reflection on its aims, purposes and outcomes. All workers need time, space, encouragement and support to think critically and reflect on their work. All training activities should have these characteristics, with specific emphasis on reflection and reviewing. Senior detached youth workers and managers with the appropriate knowledge and experience should take responsibility for leading these reviews.**

How long and how often should detached youth workers work with young people?

Very few detached youth workers work more than one or two sessions a week with any given group. Managers often blame this set-up on the need to deploy resources across many neighbourhoods, all of which have significant 'need'.

In every one of the areas visited, managers are resigned to having to spread resources more thinly than is necessary to meet those needs. This frustrates many detached youth workers:

Detached youth worker: *We often do one night here and one night there, but this is about achieving 'contacts' and not doing youth work."*

This study finds that these arrangements risk destabilising relationships with young people. Typically, the combination of a staff absence and lone-working policies means that a worker cannot contact the group. Likewise, when contact is a single session a week, young people's often-fickle movements can easily result in *their* absence. The combined effect is one of scant and *ad hoc* contact. Workers continuously attempt to renew and reinvigorate previous relationships. It is unsurprising then, that relationships (and, therefore, the potential for developmental activity) are, at best, undermined. At worst, they are irretrievably damaged. Workers scurry around trying to renew contacts whenever an event is planned. This, too, shifts the emphasis to young people opting in and out as they wish and failing to commit to the participatory dimensions of excellent detached youth work. Young people's faith and trust in workers is then eroded: a worker's absence is seen as a failure to live up to promises. The process of relationship degradation then becomes cyclic. Future youth work initiatives have to deal with young people's distrust of [new] workers. Many workers seem to be acutely aware of this paradox. Few, though, mention any concerted effort to ensure that they invest in maintaining those relationships.

Detached youth worker: *"It's important that we are not seen by people (especially young people) as a 'fly-by-night' organisation. We need to make a long-term commitment to an area."*

Where work is not enduring, those who appear to lose out most are young people with whom relationships are difficult to develop in the first place. Invariably, they distrust authority and are the most socially excluded. Once again we see how, despite social policy objectives, various systemic problems mean that, in fact, work with these young people becomes rarer still.

There is also little evidence of workers *planning* for long-term relationships with young people. Often work is deliberately short-term, because there isn't the funding for anything more enduring.

Even when work does commit to a community over the longer-term, and even when young people do therefore develop in-depth relationships with detached youth workers, a shift in project emphasis can still also have a detrimental effect on these relationships. Take the example of a young woman who had a long-term positive relationship with detached workers. They helped her deal with a range of issues and encouraged her to get involved in several activities. But the emphasis of the project then changed (when one funding stream ran out and another had to be found). Thereafter, the young woman was then involved only in the context of a sexual health outreach session. The focus of this session meant that workers could no longer work with her on *her* issues.

On the other hand, where there is a flexible approach to programme focus, young people are able, on their terms, to renew relationships where they see a need to do so. A number of detached youth workers report that young people they had previously worked with contacted them again later for support and assistance (see earlier examples in *The Importance of Relationships*). This also demonstrates how important strong and trusting relationships are within the context of a generic and enduring approach to detached youth work. Young people take with them this sense of trust and often turn to these workers for support long after their initial involvement is over.

This commitment to developing strong relationships over time has some profound (and often unanticipated) benefits in the form of reputation. A number of detached youth workers report that young people they don't know contact them on the basis of recommendations from peers who have had contact with the workers. Sometimes, they ask specifically for one worker. At others, they initiate contact with the project itself. This 'word-of-mouth' process is a particularly important way of making contact with young people who have grievances and issues with other, more formal, agencies. Short-term projects never enjoy this kind of reputation-building.

Also worthy of mention is the changing profile of young people who congregate in a given public space at any given time. Typically, groups of progressively older young people replace groups of younger ones as the evening wears on. Very few of the detached youth workers interviewed ever work after 9pm. This is a lost opportunity to engage with older young people who are often present later. The reasons given for finishing working by 9pm vary. They range from "It is simply too much to expect workers' social and family lives to be affected so much," to "It's too dangerous late at night."

Guidelines:
- **Detached youth work projects should offer young people the opportunity to have regular (and, where necessary, intensive) contact with workers. They should be planned for the longer-term and focus on a defined locality. Previous clients need to be able to renew contact as and when they need to. Staffing resources should not to be spread thinly: this erodes at the level of contact possible with young people and undermines the quality of relationships formed with them.**
- **The duration of a programme of detached youth work, while planned to be enduring, must be subject to constant scrutiny. Long-term programmes do not automatically imply benefit to young people. Nor does a project, by virtue of its long timescale alone, necessarily equate to positive learning outcomes. Detached youth workers must prepare exit strategies for work that has come to a natural end point or that is deemed to be a poor use of resources because it is not moving on. Commitment to a process that encourages young people to become informers and architects of changes in programme emphasis means that detached youth workers should always try to negotiate any changes with the young people first. But there may be times when**

even this strategy doesn't work. Ultimately, then, workers must be prepared to withdraw from groups when they judge that this is necessary, so that their resources might be invested more profitably elsewhere.

Standard:

- Detached youth work projects should be funded for a minimum of two years. They need enough resources for workers to offer contact to young people at least twice a week. In tandem, detached youth workers should be given contracts that reflect the project's commitment to relationship building. Full-time contracts are preferable. Other workers should be substantively employed (a minimum of three sessions per week, two of which are devoted to face-to-face activity with the same group).

Tackling the bureaucracy burden: monitoring, targets, recording and accrediting outcomes versus evaluation and evidence-gathering: the case for focussing on the assessment of learning

Almost all of the detached youth workers and managers interviewed express concern at the amount of bureaucracy associated with their work. Collecting and recording information is, they say, too time-consuming. And some of the processes they are expected to use are overly complex:

Detached youth worker: *"We need to be tooled up to do recording and accrediting more easily."*

They see much of the information they have to gather as of limited or no value. Its only purpose is, in their view, simply to fulfil the demands of managers and funders. Few see the collection of data as any more than 'an end in itself'. Not a single worker, and only a handful of managers (usually those with accreditation responsibilities), believe that these systems improve the quality of the work.

Part-time detached youth worker: *"After I've finished a session with young people, I've only got enough time to fill out all my monitoring forms. If I make notes that will actually be useful in my work, I have to do this in my own time."*

Several workers go further. They argue that gathering information is intrusive and puts their relationships with young people at risk. Furthermore, many detached youth workers voice concerns that the drive to record outcomes and achieve accreditation 'systematises' detached youth work to such an extent that it compromises the work's inherent flexibility.

Many managers and detached youth workers feel frustrated by the emphasis on 'achieving better outcomes'. They worry that youth work practice is under threat from a shift toward policy-makers' own views of what benefits young people. This conflicts with a practice that focuses on working with young people in order that *they* might shape this benefit. Many managers and workers say that this shift indicates a desire to control and employ detached youth work to 'sort out' a range of social problems. This, they say, undermines a form of practice that relies for its success on engaging with *young people's* agenda, not someone else's.

Many detached youth workers express concern that demands to achieve certain **targets** conflict with the need to be flexible enough to respond to the changing needs and interests of young people. Prescriptive targets, they feel, constrain the very process that sets the scene for productive work.

Guidelines:

- **Detached youth work practice should be evaluated and judged on the basis of whether it makes a difference to young people's lives.**

The test is this: does your service, your organisation, make a difference to young people?
                                                                                                Wylie (2005)

- **Young people should be central to the process of evaluation and participate in it. The significance and value of monitoring and evaluation should be discussed with them. Targets should be determined and agreed through a dialogue with young people. This is the only way to ensure that they are meaningful and relate to young people's actual (not perceived) needs.**

- **Monitoring systems should be simple and quick to use. In the early stages of developing a relationship with young people, any monitoring that they might perceive as invasive should be avoided. In these cases, workers should collect only the bare minimum of information necessary for monitoring. In some circumstances, this should be gathered by observation only. Normally this will include little more than recording sex, approximate age, ethnicity etc. Workers should not routinely solicit information about the behaviour and lifestyles of family members.**

- **Outcomes should record what happens and focus, in particular, on evidence of positive changes in young people's lives. The primary function of this information should be to shape future practice and enable young people to evaluate their own learning.**

- **The accreditation of learning must be taken as a possibility rather than a pre-scribed aim. Workers should present this as a choice and take care that it does not become a barrier to the inclusion of young people, particularly those who may have negative experiences of formality and testing in education. At all times, detached youth workers should be mindful of how the *process* of learning may help in facilitating young people's learning.**

- **Managers should be aware that setting targets *away* from the context of young people and their community – and the imperative to meet these targets – can skew the work. They must justify any targets in the light of a broader debate about the aims of detached youth work.**

- **Detached youth workers must assert the value of evidence-based practice. They should try to identify 'what works' and agree parameters for evaluation with managers, partner agencies and the young people they work with. Detached youth workers should promote evaluation** methods that befit an authentic definition of detached youth work and a commitment to participation. There should be a special emphasis on employing youth work-oriented processes to evidence learning. Processes that focus on self-assessment are most honest, useful and more related to the lived experiences of all engaged with the work. Invariably, they are also more demanding. Services should offer training and opportunities for guided reflection so that these assessment processes are productive.

- At an agency level, tools such as the NYA's 'Quality Mark' are useful. At a practice-based level, tools that encourage young people's self and peer-assessment can contribute to a much more learner-focused and qualitative framework for evaluation. Those that enable young people to chart 'the distance they have travelled' are especially enlightening, as are assessment systems based on young people's ideas.

- Workers should use lots of different media (video, art, displays etc.) and methods to engage young people' interests and encourage them to participate in assessing their learning. Plenty of useful material exists to support these endeavours. These include NYA publications such as 'Capturing the Evidence' and the 'Hear by Right' standards for participation. Ideally, workers should not adopt them wholesale as a definitive system for evaluation, but instead should use these to stimulate and complement locally negotiated assessment processes. In short, they should tailor-make systems that resonate with those they are working with.

Political dimensions of detached youth work: the significance of participation and advocacy.

Participation: *The principle that those who will be substantially affected by decisions made by social and political institutions must be involved in the making of those decisions.*

The study found precious little evidence of a systematic commitment to young people's participation beyond encouraging them to get involved in activities. Indeed, the concept of participation was rarely understood in terms other than young people 'taking part'. This calls into question the effectiveness of wider youth service planning to increase young people's participation. Training in participation, where it has occurred (and this is rare) tends to focus on learning to consult young people on specific themes, often at the behest of partner agencies. Likewise, many of the handbooks and 'participatory resources' available to workers offer little guidance on how to support young people in creating their own youth service experience.

The bureaucratic burden explored above is a further barrier to participation. The prescription of youth work programmes fundamentally contradicts the rationale behind a meaningful vision of participation, in which the process of programme development and assessment emanates from the young people.

There is limited evidence of detached youth workers systematically advocating on behalf of young people. Area forums and the like often, simplistically, blame young people for problems in the community. If a youth worker is not there to speak up for young people, there will rarely be anyone else to diffuse the antagonism.

> **Guidelines:**
> - Based on the definitions developed above, detached youth work is intrinsically a democratic form of practice. Young people have the right to influence, if not wholly determine, the terms of their engagement. Where this does not happen, this is not authentic youth work. It has more in common with leisure provision. The theory and practice of detached youth work must therefore be considered in these and wider political terms. Advocating on behalf of young people is a political act. Supporting young people so that they can speak up for themselves requires detached youth workers to see their work in terms of its contribution to young people's political education. The training of detached youth workers needs to reflect this.

Promotion

All agencies recognise the value of promoting their services. Few, though, make any strategic attempts to do this. Most rely on effective networking within partnership settings, as these are seen as the environment in which decisions about resource allocation are made.

All agencies appreciate the value of media coverage for their work though, again, their commitment to achieving this varied.

Some agencies receive favourable recognition of their mobile provision, which appears to suggest that there is political capital in being 'visible'. Typically, members of the local community or councillors will contact the service and say, for example, "it was good to see your bus on the estate." Clearly, it is important to differentiate between the gains to be made from 'visibility' and the value of the work that actually takes place. While these are clearly not incompatible, detached youth work does not intrinsically lend itself to visibility. Nor, in some senses, should it. It is possible that the relative invisibility of detached youth workers is why some young people choose to engage with them. This is true particularly of those who are most socially excluded and sensitive about 'them & us' issues and authority. So efforts to attract young people to the service by promoting it through visibility may, unwittingly, achieve precisely the opposite.

There are parallels in the increasing prevalence of uniforms for detached youth workers. Almost all of the detached projects visited have some kind of uniform. These have value in terms of health and safety; they, for example, protect in bad weather. And some workers feel that wearing a uniform means that they are less likely to be challenged [or even assaulted] by members of the community who, even if they don't know the workers themselves, may recognise the uniform. Other detached youth workers, though, are uncomfortable about being seen to be 'one of the establishment'. They argue that wearing a uniform may, in fact, undermine their ability to engage with those 'hard-to-reach'. They argue that being known by the wider community by name is what makes them safe, rather than their [a] uniform. Finally, *some* young people who live in more hostile areas feel that a uniform gives *them* confidence – they feel that they can trust the people wearing them.

> **Guideline:**
> - Promotional activities designed to promote detached youth work and the wider youth service should not do so at the expense of good practice. A 'youth service van', for example, may indeed give the youth service a 'public face'. But this may make detached youth workers less flexible. They end up waiting for young people to come to them / the van, instead of going out to seek contact on the young people's own turf. Undoubtedly, the best way for detached youth workers to promote their work is to get themselves known in the community. This is more likely to happen as a result of community conversations, rather than wearing badges and uniforms. Being embedded in a community and knowing all its members gives the detached youth worker an authority based on respect. All detached youth workers should aim to be known in this way. Uniforms are no short cut.

Infrastructure: Base & administrative support

The detached youth work visited for this research is based in a range of buildings. These include youth centres, young people's centres and the administrative bases of children's and young people's services. Some detached youth workers have their own space. Others share with various other officers. A few don't have any identifiable base. Some detached youth workers have dedicated administrative support; some have none and are responsible for all their own administration. Some workers have the use of computers; some have no access to the internet or email. A significant number of workers lacked the IT skills to do their own administration efficiently and no training had been given to address this issue.

Workers with a central base enjoy valuable support and networking with colleagues. Invariably, though, 'hot-desking' arrangements exist, particularly for part-time workers, which is far from ideal. One disadvantage of centrally located bases, though, is that detached youth workers often have to travel significant distances to work with young people. For those working in rural areas, this seems unavoidable. This makes it difficult for detached youth workers to be intimately connected with the areas in which they work. It's easier for those who are based in the area in which they work to raise their local profile. Detached youth workers, will, for example, interact with members of the community (especially adults) every day, on the street and in local shops, in and out of working hours. This roots the project in the community. Detached youth workers can get to know their patches through their everyday movements. This can lead to them being able to access a wide range of local resources such as sponsorship and equipment etc. Becoming a 'local worker' also facilitates young people's access to these resources.

If detached youth workers are based in youth centres, young people find it much more difficult to differentiate between what the detached youth workers do and what centre-based workers do. The research finds that this differentiation is important. Workers aligned too closely to youth centres may be tempted to work with young people who attend youth clubs on the nights that the youth centres are closed. This defeats one of the objects of detached youth work, which is to work with young people whom don't access centre-based provision. Young people – especially if they are barred from that provision – may then be overlooked more than ever.

> **Guidelines:**
> - **Excellent detached youth work depends on a well-resourced infrastructure. It is essential for detached youth workers to have a dedicated office base with dedicated administrative support (specifically allied to the project), so that they can plan and reflect on their work and do their administration efficiently. If necessary, managers must provide appropriate IT training.**
> - **More subtly, projects should have a distinct and discreet identity to distinguish them from other youth work provision. Ideally, they should not be based in youth centres, so that they can assert and maintain their independence.**

Funding

Many of the current funding regimes for detached youth work are woefully inadequate. All managers identified funding as a permanent cause for concern. For many, daily work often focuses on the challenge of finding resources to maintain service levels, keep workers in post and, where possible, develop new provision to meet the many demands upon the service. Most managers feel they have no choice but to accept offers of funding, even when the work this would pay for does not truly reflect their own vision of what counts as detached youth work. This conflict is heightened further by the fact that most funding regimes are short-term. Managers feel trapped in a seemingly endless and time-consuming pattern of trying to find fresh funding.

Detached youth work manager: *"We are forced to take money off funders because we are starving."*

Many managers are dismayed that their efforts to attract new resources force them to engage with a social policy agenda (which, in turn, informs the availability of resources) that clashes with their vision of genuine detached youth work.

Detached youth work manager: *"The state puts up money that meets their agenda; this is different from our wish to respond to young people's agenda."*

Contracting arrangements, especially those that fund project-oriented work, create a significant dilemma for detached youth workers and their managers. There is, many say, a conflict between a focus on 'projects' and a more holistic vision of detached youth work – in which work develops on the basis of dialogue and negotiation with young people. As has been seen, some workers try to 'square this circle' by linking funding up with young people who they *already know* to have particular interests, on the basis of prior relationships. Conversely, some managers speak positively of the clarity that contracting arrangements bring. The managers know exactly what they have to achieve, where, and by when. Rarely, though, do the detached youth workers see this as positive.

Funding arrangements appear to drive the 'pre-scription' of a great deal of detached youth work. Resources are often available for project-based activities that focus on issues and problems of concern to funders. Some detached youth workers see these as doing "something different" from detached youth work. They find this frustrating – projects rolled out in this way, with little regard for whether young people want them, don't fit a more principled vision of detached youth work. Funding to work in *this* way is rarely available.

These tensions are more acute when funding regimes are short-term (and this is common). What emerges is a series of short-term, *ad hoc* activities, many of which are issue-based and programme-oriented. Some detached youth workers say they have to "ring the changes" even though what they need is to continue with existing work. For example, sexual health initiatives have been set up in areas despite workers identifying the primary problem as antisocial behaviour caused by lack of leisure provision for young people. Similarly, funding is often available through local Crime and Disorder Partnerships, provided the work has this emphasis.

Most detached youth workers feel that this culture of short-term funding, high funder expectations and a prescription to deliver specific outcomes on specific agendas within a short time period has a major impact on the quality of the work. It shifts detached youth work, they say, from an open-ended process to one characterised by the delivery of programmes that often fail to resonate with young people.

The study also finds many funding regimes also impose a significant **bureaucratic burden** on detached youth workers. Funders typically want detailed monitoring information, which is time-consuming for workers. As a result, detached youth workers spend more time on administration and therefore less engaged in face-to-face work with young people. Increased financial turnover, ironically, chips away at contact with young people. More money is accessed, but less work is done by those who are most skilled – senior workers – who become consumed in producing the paperwork expected by funders. Some agencies consider this an unacceptable outcome. They ignore or reject funding opportunities in order to protect the integrity of their face-to-face work.

Funding regimes are also often fickle, shifting from one area to another depending on the priorities identified by partnership arrangements. Detached youth workers have trouble identifying long-term resources for particular communities. And keeping workers in an area for extended periods of time (so that they might build strong relationships with young people and the wider community), becomes difficult. Often, then, detached youth work adopts a 'leap-frogging' approach. It follows funding opportunities from one community to another. Many managers do this in order to maintain service levels, though they are aware that it compromises the service's ability to do good work.

> **Guidelines:**
> - Excellent detached youth work is, invariably, underwritten by core funding. In a local authority context, this implies the need for mainstream funding. This funding should, wherever possible, be ring-fenced for detached youth work. This is essential to ensuring that detached youth workers and managers have enough authority to commit resources to a model of flexible working. Without this, the quality of detached youth work will always be undermined. Managers must promote investment in flexible, process-oriented practice as the mechanism by which detached youth work contributes most significantly to the wider social policy agenda.

Management

The study found no consistent management pattern for detached youth work. Some detached youth workers feel that their managers are distant. Others report a high level of support. Some workers see managers as "part of the problem". Others see them as "fighting their corner":

Detached youth worker: *"Managers have got lost; they need to fight back and be advocates of detached youth work much more."*

Detached youth worker: *"Service managers need to set and defend boundaries, to allow workers to get on with the work. They need to say 'this is what we [the detached youth workers] are doing, and why'. Managers need to explain the reasoning behind detached youth work."*

Detached youth worker: *"We're fortunate that our Principal Officer gives us great support, especially in ensuring funding opportunities take on our values as detached youth workers."*

A number of managers have a sophisticated understanding of what detached youth work is. Often this is because they had once been detached youth workers themselves. The managers therefore often represent an important body of knowledge and experience (particularly with respect to process-oriented ways of working). However, there is little evidence of them using their experience in a strategic way to support the professional development of junior staff, many of whom are part-time and haven't had much training. Few managers schedule time to go out with their detached youth workers and engage directly with face-to-face work. The most common explanation is that time-consuming administrative duties prevent them from being able to offer more direct, practice-based support.

Many part-time detached youth workers complain about the lack of supervision they receive, in terms of both an opportunity to discuss day-to-day practice and also to reflect on their professional development. In some agencies, this amounts to as little as a few hours each year. This clearly compromises the quality of detached youth work and the potential for learning (particularly in terms of passing on knowledge and experience). For many part-time detached youth workers, contact with senior colleagues is the most significant way for them to learn to do good work. It is clear that almost all part-time staff desperately need this kind of support. The 'drive for delivery' cuts the time available to learn.

> **Guideline:**
> - The effective management of detached youth work is undoubtedly challenging. Managers must ensure that detached youth workers focus on practice. Managers must, therefore, take primary responsibility for engaging with the partnership structures that now inform a great deal of detached youth work. To do this effectively, managers must have close contact with detached youth workers and the communities they work with. They can then act as a *conduit* for local issues and refer problems back to partnership structures. Managers must pay close attention to staff feedback. This should not be limited to staff meetings: managers should also make regular practice observation visits where they can engage with the workers, and indeed with young people, in a practice setting. This contact is essential for managers to 'keep in touch' with what is happening on the ground. It is also vital as a means of monitoring and supporting the professional development of staff (including through 'on the hoof' mentoring). And it means that managers can then relay the realities of face-to-face practice back to partner agencies and funders, who, without such knowledge, may fail to appreciate the subtleties of effective practice. For part-timers, this level of manager involvement is essential.

Staffing

Detached youth work has a long history of employing part-time workers. Many contribute enormously to the overall impact of the project. Significantly, this study finds that many of the part-timers come from the local community. They bring with them a knowledge of 'the street' and of the local community that few non-indigenous workers possess. Many have instinctive communicative abilities based on years of immersion in local culture and language. And many have life experiences similar to the young people they work with. These strengths are often instrumental in the project developing relationships with local young people.

But the study finds that many of these workers lack theoretical knowledge. In part, weak **training** regimes are to blame. But, some at least, lack support in examining the local cultures that inform their perspectives. Typically, there might be a negative disposition toward formal learning. Some youth workers emerge from the ranks of those who were themselves disaffected from learning. Workers who are encouraged to process their experiences can add tremendous value to their more instinctive abilities.

The research also finds that these experiences, though, make many of these youth workers uncomfortable about training. They may not be interested in becoming professionally qualified. This appears to be a reality for almost all projects. The more positive managers emphasise the value of coaching, mentoring and guided informal discussion. But this is difficult in services where the ratio of part-time to full-time workers is high (in some case 10:1).

Many agencies have significant problems recruiting and retaining staff. This problem is exacerbated by short-term funding programmes: workers are constantly worried about their job security. Typically, as a short-term funding stream nears its end, staff look for work elsewhere. Ironically, managers often find new funds only to face a staff shortage because workers have left. This leads to an unproductive scenario: time, funding and other resources are constantly consumed in an endless round of attempting to secure funding *and* recruit staff.

High staff turnover also makes it difficult to organise a coherent and sequential **training** programme. New staff join the service on a regular basis, making it difficult to organise professional training that is appropriate for all. Economies of scale mean that particular training courses are then run as and when there are enough people to make them viable. Workers who join the service just *after* one of these courses may have to wait many months to receive training. There is also the phenomenon of workers being forced to do training in the wrong sequence – for example, doing a detached youth work course *before* one on generic youth work. Together, these factors undermine workers' learning and professional development. Inevitably, this puts many quality candidates off committing to the youth service in the first place.

The study finds day-to-day recruitment problems in the wider youth service, including of professionally qualified workers. Where staffing problems exist, managers often treat centre-based youth work as a priority. Some detached youth workers say they are told to cover for absent centre-based colleagues. This relegates detached youth work to the status of poor relation. The upshot of this is that contact with young people who don't go to centres is broken. And relationships with those young people are invariably undermined – and sometimes lost for good.

Guideline:
- **The culture of an over-emphasis on part-time working must be scrutinised. It is clear that a detached youth worker who works just one or two sessions a week will be under pressure to commit almost all this time to working with young people. This is understandable. But this, then, severely limits the time available for training and supervision, both of which underpin excellent detached work. Unless workers do this in their own time (i.e. voluntarily), or unless extra funding to support this can be found (and this assumes their availability to train), employing detached youth workers for only one or two sessions a week is incompatible with excellent practice. More substantive contracts are the only way to retain a significant face-to-face input *and* provide time for reflection, managerial supervision and training. Project managers and those with responsibility for resource allocation should, in their financial planning, acknowledge this. Furthermore, they should commit, wherever possible, to a team-based approach. They need at least one full-time or substantive professionally trained worker who, alongside managers, supports part-time staff.**

'Fit'

There is little evidence of a concerted attempt to ensure 'fit' between different elements of the youth service to ensure that all young people can access services how and when they want.

> **Guideline:**
> - **Youth service managers must scrutinise and plan for a coherent overall 'fit' of youth work activities so that the needs of all young people are met. The marriage of all elements means detached youth workers can refer young people to different projects, as appropriate. Implicitly, detached youth work must be differentiated from other forms of practice and accorded its own status. Resources for detached youth work should ideally be ring-fenced. Staff should not be treated as a flexible resource to cover, for example, the absences of centre-based staff.**

Partnership working (detached youth work perspective)

The value of partnership

Partnership working offers many potential benefits. Many detached youth workers mention how working with others increases opportunities and resources available to young people. Typically, detached youth workers see partnerships as good for 'networking'. They find out who else they might be able to refer young people to, and where they themselves might go for support and resources.

These benefits cannot, though, be taken for granted; in some circumstances, there are potential detrimental consequences of partnerships.

Detached youth workers, particularly those of longer standing, argue that they always have, of their own initiative, sought out others to work with. Today, they are increasingly obliged to do so; they find this frustrating. Previously, they would work with others – through informal negotiations – on the basis of their own judgement about what would be best for young people. They feel concerned that today's culture of detached youth work now expects and assumes that they will work in partnership with all. Many associate partnership working with endless **bureaucracy**. Their time, they judge, would very often be better spent getting on with face-to-face work.

Some workers report an attitude from partners of: 'you are in partnership with us so you must…'. They feel that excessive formality conflicts with their own way of working, which pivots on informal negotiation and mutual respect for professional autonomy. A number of workers complain that they are, in short, told with whom they should work in partnership. In the past, informal contacts were seen as most appropriate. Today, those relationships have become formalised. There are various consequences of this. Detached youth workers are now, for example, expected to share information with those partners, even when this conflicts with the confidentiality implied by their work – and even, on occasion, with their pledges to young people.

Some detached youth workers feel exasperated by the 'fundamentalism' of partnership arrangements. They have their doubts about whether these arrangements focus explicitly on improving benefits and outcomes for young people. Partnerships, they say, are simply places where other agencies seek to coerce detached youth workers into meeting *their* (the agency's) targets, without fully analysing how these might be interpreted 'on the ground'. Some detached youth workers are concerned that partners' interpretations of specific social policy agendas conflict with their own agendas – and, indeed, the interests of the young people they work with.

Detached youth work manager: *"What the community calls 'Community Safety' is what young people call 'getting the police off my back'."*

Detached youth worker: *"We have to realise that putting young people at the heart of our work might not enamour us to others – but it is our job. We have to be prepared to say: 'I am not here for this; I am here for young people'."*

By contrast, others are concerned that 'direct delivery' has become such a priority that there is little opportunity to engage in [any] partnership work. Managers often veto meeting with other agencies. This means there is little chance of, for example, engaging in much-needed community development activities with local neighbourhood forums or tenants' and residents' committees.

Promoting understanding: facilitating partners' learning

Many of those interviewed express a strong interest in the potential outcomes of the research process and how this might help promote a wider understanding of detached work within partnership settings. This reflects a general concern that the lack of a coherent picture of detached youth work undermines efforts to champion their work:

Detached youth work manager: *"We need help in getting others to understand what detached youth work is all about. A substantive piece of research will back up our efforts to do this."*

Senior manager: *"The most important thing we hope to get from the PIN is a strong definition of what detached youth work is ... we are really struggling to develop the understanding of partners as to what it is."*

Partnership working: partners' perspective

Interviews with those working for partnership agencies suggest that there is, indeed, a widespread lack of understanding about what detached youth work is, or of its underpinning values. Some betray an almost complete lack of knowledge about such work. The only people with a sophisticated understanding of detached youth work have, almost without exception, been involved in it at some stage in their career (usually as detached youth workers themselves). Despite this, most of those interviewed express great interest in detached youth work.

Partners also express their own criticisms. Many feel that some detached youth workers are not committed to working with them or have reneged on pledges to do so. Sometimes this is based on the assumption that detached youth workers could *make* young people available to [these] other agencies. Often, partners envisage that detached youth workers will take on the job of keeping discipline during the young people's experience of another provision. Few officers of partner agencies appreciate that detached youth workers are themselves already involved in a range of activities, many pre-planned, and that they can't always therefore be around to help. Equally, few appreciate that the young people's involvement needs to be negotiated with them. This said, there is some evidence of these challenges being overcome. Usually this is as a result of a meaningful dialogue or due to detached youth workers *initiating* contact because they believe that working with a partner agency can meets needs that have emerged from their work with young people.

More strategically, the partnership experiences of some detached youth workers illustrate the benefits of more coherent resource planning and service-provision. Typically, a range of youth work providers (statutory and voluntary) collaborate on major events, conferences and holiday programmes. This extends choice to young people.

The study finds evidence of some excellent practice in which detached youth workers are able to help partner agencies that find it difficult to access specific groups of young people. For example, a worker from a sexual health drop-in project (to which no one was 'dropping-in' (sic.)) accompanied detached youth workers on a number of street-based sessions. By talking to potential clients, the project worker found out a great deal about the lives of young people and what stops them from accessing services. The worker was then able to change the project to make it more accessible to young people.

This process involved far more than a member of another agency simply accompanying detached youth workers on the street. The detached youth workers in question took time to explain exactly what detached youth work was and what their work entailed. They also worked out exactly what the other agency hoped to get out of the visits, and agreed protocols for their involvement. They worked hard to ensure that others did not treat their experience of going out with detached youth workers as, as one senior worker put it, "a trip to the zoo". This shows attention to detail, an appreciation of ethical considerations and a willingness to support other agencies so that services became much more widely accessible to young people. It is an excellent example of how partnership working can really benefit young people.

Guidelines:
- **All those involved in detached youth work must have a clear vision of what they do, so that they can support partner agencies in developing an in-depth understanding of detached youth work. Partnership work depends on it.**
- **It is essential to clarify the roles of and relationships between partner agencies – particularly as increasing numbers of non-detached youth work practitioners work on the streets with young people. This means that detached youth workers, too, will need to explore their own**

> role with young people. Young people need to know what detached youth workers are, what they represent, and how they differ from the other agencies with which they might come into contact on the street.
>
> - Two essential questions should be explored if partnership work is to be effective. First, 'What is the issue / problem?' Second, "What is the most appropriate response?" Partnerships must take a holistic view of what needs to be done and how the partnership itself can promote positive outcomes. Youth service managers should aim for this more enlightened position – and resist the more narrow default view that detached youth work can somehow always be shoe-horned in to whatever project is going. Managers must argue one key fundamental: that detached youth work must play an *appropriate* role.
> - Partnerships must be scrutinised for how, exactly, they benefit young people; it cannot be assumed that they always do.

Training

All partner agencies believe that detached youth workers should be well trained. But translating this commitment into practice is another matter. The level of training for detached youth workers varies widely across the partner agencies. In some cases, full-time detached youth workers have no professional qualifications, even though job descriptions demand them. Often, there is a caveat: workers who were previously part-timers are 'supported' to achieve these qualifications. But the fact remains that many detached youth workers, though poorly trained, are expected to work to the same standards as their professionally qualified counterparts. The implications of this are obvious. The attention to detail that is required for excellent practice is often absent. When part-time staff significantly outnumber full-timers, capacity is further weakened, see **staffing**.

The training of part-time workers is particularly worrying. Some part-time detached youth workers have not been trained either in youth work or in detached youth work. As described in **staffing** above, they may have what might be described as 'instinctive' abilities. But excellent practice can never happen on the basis of this alone. Training must build on these abilities:

Detached youth work manager: *"Part-timers need support to develop skills in detached youth work: they need all the help they can get."*

Specific detached youth work training regimes vary from in-depth specialist training to no more than a couple of sessions. While all services articulate the need for good training in detached youth work, their attitudes about how to achieve this ranged enormously. One agency took the view that all youth workers need to be trained in all forms of youth work, including detached youth work, principally to ensure the service could be as "flexible as possible". This was reflected in the service's generic job descriptions. This service's detached youth workers had, however, received no more than two days' training in detached youth work and spoke of being moved from one section of the service to another.

Other partners, by contrast, see detached youth work as a specialism. Job descriptions reflect this position and workers benefit by getting more in-depth training tailored to their specific needs and roles. Flexible training models, while not intrinsically poor in their own right, tend to provide fewer opportunities for the professional development of detached youth workers.

Despite a wholesale appreciation of the value of training for staff development, few agencies have strong and well-resourced training programmes for detached youth workers. In some cases, the demand to 'deliver' has now become so all-consuming that there seems to be little time or inclination to organise training. This particularly affects part-time detached youth workers. Training can take them 'off the job' for significant periods of time. As a result, training opportunities are sometimes not made readily accessible to them. A failure to upskill staff compromises the quality of the work. In some circumstances, this extends to managerial veto of community development activities in favour of face-to-face work. Working with young people should always be the priority, but it should not exist to the exclusion of training and community development / networking activities. Managers need to find a way to balance all of these activities in a way that, ultimately, improves practice and, thereby, benefits young people.

Guidelines:

- **Managers have a duty of care for all workers. But they must take particular responsibility for those who have had limited training or experience or who have recently become professionally qualified. For them, it may be appropriate for the manager to plan a staged progression of engagement and experience. The worker would, initially, work with less challenging groups, in order to increase his or her confidence. They should never be thrown into the 'lion's den'. Managers should assess the skills and abilities of workers during induction and throughout training. This will ensure that staff only do work that is appropriate for their level of professional development. They must negotiate the parameters of this work with the workers themselves, set them out clearly and stick to them. This allows workers to make professional judgements about the level of risk implied by their activities. Typically, (albeit rarely), experienced practitioners may decide they can engage positively with young people who are involved in dangerous activities such as violent gang activity or even drug and gun crime. The worker will have considerable experience and will have built up a strong reputation in the local area. This should certainly not be expected of all. But it represents the crucial importance of worker autonomy, as distinct from external directives. Training regimes should encourage both this professional autonomy and also an appreciation of personal limitations. That way, workers will become skilled in analysis (including of their own skills and abilities), decision-making and assessing support available from other agencies. See also comments made in** *Reflection, Reviewing and Analysis.*
- **Issue-based training should emerge from the findings of community profiles. For example, detached youth workers working in areas of high drug use should get training on this. This should not, however, imply that drug-use (or whatever) is the only thing that needs to be worked on. Instead, detached youth workers will be able to draw upon this training as and when the topic of drugs emerges during dialogue with young people. In no circumstances should detached**

youth workers make 'drug-use' the sole basis of their conversations with young people.

Standards:

- Detached youth workers must first be trained in the generic aspects of youth work, since these are elemental to all youth work practice. This training must take place in the right sequence – i.e. first an induction, then generic youth work training, then specialist training in detached youth work. Specialist training should include exploration of the values, history, definitions, aims and methodologies associated with detached youth work.

- Regular opportunities for training (both formal and informal) are essential for continuous professional development. Engaging with other detached youth workers at regional and national events and conferences is part of this. These opportunities should be available to all those involved in detached youth work.

WIDER CONTEXTUAL ISSUES

Social policy context

This research finds that, in many senses, detached youth work has lost its way. It is more about meeting the needs of young people *as defined by adults and policy-makers* rather than as defined by young people themselves. Simply speaking, what drives it now are the needs of adults, not those of young people. There is no clearer example of this than in the context of the antisocial behaviour agenda. Here, an 'off the street' mentality recruits detached youth work to meet the perceived needs of adults in the community, instead of those of the local young people.

This study finds that where good practice in detached youth work does exist it does so despite of, rather than because of, the social policy context. Many of the bureaucratic dimensions associated with this context are deleterious to good practice. The study therefore concludes that excellent detached youth work is not possible in this context. The study reveals a historical tendency for detached youth workers to 'bend' (or subvert) social policy parameters in order to secure the greatest benefit for young people. This 'space for subversion' has shrunk to such an extent that detached youth workers' 'room for manoeuvre' is increasingly restricted. Ironically, this deprives them of the very flexibility that has, until now, been the hallmark of effective practice.

Detached youth work continues to have the potential for doing good work with young people. But this potential is both under-exploited and hampered by aspects of the context in which it now operates. A failure to learn from the past, coupled with unrealistic expectations, means that resources for detached youth work are often wasted. If those concerned want to bolster the morale of detached youth workers and revive a spirit of vocationalism, they must be prepared to revisit the essential aims and values that underpin detached youth work. More enlightened policy and an enhanced funding regime is needed. Without these commitments, detached youth work will never fulfil its true potential.

Young people need better outcomes – that much, no one disputes. And the commitment to provide services to young people should broadly be celebrated. However, the mechanisms for achieving these outcomes, as envisioned by policy-makers, don't support effective practice; they get in its way:

Detached youth work manager: *"Transforming Youth Work is good for entitlement but bad for bureaucracy."*

Detached youth work faces many challenges. Some of these actually threaten its very identity and *raison d'etre*. Conflicts focus on the context in which the work takes place. The formalisation of much practice is at odds with a form of practice that centres on young people's voluntary participation. Progress depends on respecting and engaging with young people's view of the world (and what they think would help them). The art of detached youth work is to encourage young people to explore – through dialogue – a range of perspectives that can help them distinguish 'needs' from 'wants'. Any attempt to prescribe this vision is doomed to failure. It also undermines the democratic credentials of detached youth work. A way of working that has a pre-ordained end-point erodes the very real potential young people have to become autonomous adults and active citizens. Indeed, where young people, through this process, decide on a particular life path, then this too must be respected. Any profitable relationship depends on this.

There are important philosophical questions to be asked about how far detached youth work should seek to market itself. Clearly, establishing a coherent and well understood identity is important. But its history of being in productive tension with many state apparatus begs, in today's context, questions about its incorporation and shifting value base. The evidence from this research suggests that this shift damages effective practice, especially with young people who are socially excluded.

The challenge for detached youth work is to explore how two agendas (those of young people and those of policy-makers) can simultaneously be engaged where they differ. Both should be made as transparent as possible. This is an essential step to clarifying where (and where not) detached youth work might work, without compromising its authenticity. This transparency will mean that not all interventions will be found to be ethically justifiable. It will, though, allow detached youth workers to engage with different agendas positively and argue in favour of evidence-based practice.

There is, without doubt, a need for a proper dialogue about funding and the potential for ring-fencing funding for detached youth work. The study finds that a distinctive contribution must be supported by distinctive funding. Excellence will also have to be paid for. Too few projects are adequately resourced. And too few have access to long-term flexible funding streams, without which their effectiveness is also compromised.

The importance of professional autonomy

This research reveals that excellence is most likely to be in evidence when detached youth work is mainstream funded. This gives detached youth workers greater autonomy and control over resources. More crucially, it allows them to make the day-to-day decisions about how and where they work. This increases the likelihood that practice will focus on the needs of young people, rather than the demands of others.

The context of partnership working also demands scrutiny. This is particularly true where political imperatives are cascaded down to youth service managers through funding and commissioning mechanisms. If the demands of others conflict with the needs of young people, managers must prioritise young people's needs. Strong deployment rationales and community profiling activities will support them in this.

The demands for detached youth work far outstrip its capacity. Detached youth work providers therefore have to decide how to use their limited resources. This is nothing new. But the many demands now constrain traditionally autonomous decision-making processes. These demands are complex. They are often overly influenced by the 'power brokers' within partnership arrangements, who control funding. Good practice depends on elevating the status of detached youth work within partnerships, so that it is not seen as a poor relation. Doing this requires commitment and **promotion**.

Does process-oriented work face extinction?

The *outcomes* of detached youth work are of interest to all, and an obsession of many. "Achieving better outcomes" is the mantra. And so it should be. But this study finds that many of those with an interest in detached youth work have limited understanding of – or scant regard for – the importance of the detached youth work *process* in achieving positive outcomes. The 'pre-scription' of outcomes fundamentally contradicts and undermines this process. In its stead are more and more examples of programme-led work. This, too, clashes with a way of working that is distinctive precisely *because* it is young people that inform and lead it. Detached youth work often represents their *only* opportunity to learn, through experience, the knowledge, skills and attitudes necessary to be an autonomous adult.

Work that is fuelled by the attitude that there is a *problem* that needs to be *solved*, or that has an issue-related programme that needs to be delivered, will never fit an authentic definition of detached youth work. To think like this means to always see young people as *the problem* – one that *needs fixing*.

Internalisation

This study reveals that many are concerned that detached youth work is losing its way. Those who express this most strongly are those with experience of working in less prescribed ways. Of particular concern are the narratives of newer detached youth workers (especially part-timers) who have had limited training. These workers seem to have internalised the culture of pre-scribed programmes so deeply that they aren't even aware that there ever could, or should be, an alternative way of working. The new era of targets, recorded outcomes and accreditation is now so prevalent that visions of effective practice now have more in common with school than with youth work.

The demands of management clearly contribute to this. But it is the wider context of what detached youth work is and has become that informs this perspective. The cultural history of progressive, democratic pedagogy no longer exists. It has succumbed to interventions that are more concerned about behaviour management and control than they are about the education and welfare of young people. Young people may also be starting to internalise this culture – some now demand accreditation for everything. Fundamentally, these social forces illustrate how youth work values have been subject to reinvention. This research reveals that youth work, by any authentic definition, is increasingly unrecognisable. It shows how many of those who claim to champion detached youth work are becoming mere by-standers in its demise. As with all educators, detached youth workers must examine their value base. They must commit to a vision of the society they want to live in and work for.

Social exclusion

The study finds that detached youth workers work with fewer socially excluded young people. This may be a product of deliberate attempts to hit 'reach' targets. A culture that values contact above relationships has no time for the slow, methodical process of getting to know those who are challenging to work with. Detached youth work (and indeed its funders) faces a stark choice. If it truly wants to work effectively with young people who are socially excluded, it must work in a different way – and to different 'targets'. The irony is that the social policy agenda is contradictory. Its rhetoric articulates a zeal to work with these young people. But its use of bureaucracy (primarily, its seems, to promote accountability) smothers effective practice.

ENDPIECE

The research finds that an authentic vision of detached youth work is disappearing, taking with it the vital skills and attitudes that make good detached youth work possible. This report identifies the detail of these skills and attitudes. This, it is hoped, will act as a stimulus for a future, more authentic vision of what excellent detached youth work is. As a document it can do no more than record findings. In the longer term, authentic detached youth work will exist only if there is a concerted effort to build an alliance for its survival.

This research should shed some light on what detached youth work is, and on the distinctive contribution it can make. In particular, the study finds, detached youth work is, for many young people, the only chance they have truly to shape their own education. It is this opportunity to learn through the practice of democracy that is its most distinctive and potentially powerful contribution – not just for the young people it works with, but wider society. A commitment to participation demands that this opportunity exists for all and is actively encouraged.

By sharing the elements of excellent practice witnessed during this research, this report constructs a picture of what excellent detached youth work can and should look like.

It is no coincidence that there are more guidelines than standards. The guidelines are designed to stimulate thinking and promote good judgement-making. This is the lifeblood of excellent detached youth work. Standards provide the foundations and should be incontrovertible. Together they should enhance the day-to-day practice of detached youth workers and support managers in their efforts to promote a wider understanding of detached youth work to partner agencies. To do so, they must assert a more authentic definition of detached youth work. Ultimately, all those involved in detached youth work must make the case that such a definition is essential if the work is to be effective in reaching out to young people, many of whom have precious little contact with other services.

The report identifies a number of barriers to excellence that arise from the wider social policy context in which detached youth work is now firmly located. The concern (and irony) here is that this diminishes its ability to work with those specifically identified in social policy. Excellent detached youth work is not possible in this context. Detached youth work must redefine itself if it is to do justice to its history, aims and values and, more importantly, to the young people it was designed to work with.

As one manager commented: *"We need a vision, so detached youth workers know where the work started and where they are going. Disciples are needed to promote this vision."*

This document should act as an endorsement to those who seek to articulate an authentic vision of detached youth work on a day-to-day basis. It should be a useful and powerful tool to support internal service reviews. This will help clarify what detached youth workers should be doing –

and how. Detached youth workers and their managers can then promote a wider and deeper understanding of what they do to, not only to those who undertake and manage the work, but also to external partners, funders, policy-makers, the wider public *and* young people.

Today's culture often lends uncritical support for innovatory practice. This study, by contrast, finds that promoting excellence today has more to do with 'dusting off' and reinvigorating historical models and processes. Success, it shows, will have more to do with 'going back to basics' than with trying something new. What will be different today is how those 'basics' are used to engage with the changing dimensions of youth culture, as determined by young people.

Paradoxically, the features that define detached youth work are under great threat, but also fundamental to best practice. What has been learnt here about detached youth work is, in a sense, significant for the future of youth work in general. Detached youth work, as with youth work generally, is distinctive because of its fundamental commitment to respecting young people's voluntary engagement and their right to inform the terms and substance of their engagement. Starting from a position of respect for young people's lifestyle choices, however unpalatable to some, is essential to developing relationships with young people. Out of these relationships, change is possible.

For many young people, detached youth work offers the only opportunity they have to learn through the exercise of *their* power how to make decisions that can enable them to become autonomous and flourishing adults. This experiential form of political and democratic education is noticeably absent within the wide array of 'opportunities' extended to young people today.

The world of youth work has moved on. It is now much more explicitly based in a wider social policy context. Undoubtedly, the contemporary social policy agenda brings many challenges. But equally, the fact that detached youth work is identified as a contributor gives it the chance to play a key role in supporting young people. But for this to happen, detached youth work must focus on the needs of young people. And it must make the value of doing so clear to all stakeholders. Then it can claim to be authentic and, implicitly, of benefit to young people and wider society.

Graeme A. Tiffany, **2007**

References

Arnold, J., Askins, D., Davies, R., Evans, S., Rogers, A. and Taylor, T. (1981) *The Management of Detached Work. How and Why*. Leicester: National Association of Youth Clubs.

Burgess, M. and Burgess, I. (2006) *Don't Shoot! I'm a Detached Youth Worker*. Lyme Regis: Russel House Publishing.

Butler, S. (2005) *Detached Youth Work: Findings from inspections. New Framework 2004*. Presentation at Oldham Detached Youth Work conference, 29th January 2005.

Crimmens, D., Factor, F., Jeffs, T., Pitts, J., Pugh, C., Spence, J. and Truner, P. (2004) *Reaching socially excluded young people: A national study of street-based youth work*. Leicester: Joseph Rowntree Foundation.

Davies, B. (2001) *Background: the development of detached and outreach work with young people*. Unpublished.

Davies, B. and Docking, J. (2004) *TraNSForming Lives: Re-engaging young people through community-based projects*. DfES.

Department for Education and Employment (2001) *Transforming Youth Work. Developing youth work for young people*, London: Department for Education and Employment / Connexions.

HMSO (1960) *The Youth Service in England and Wales (The Albermarle Report)*. London: HMSO.

Joseph Rowntree Foundation (2004) http://www.jrf.org.uk/knowledge/findings/costings/664.asp.

National Youth Agency *yqsm Quality Mark for Services for Young People*. http://www.nya.org.uk/Templates/internal.asp?NodeID=90871.

Comfort, H., Merton, B., Payne, M. and Flint, W. (2006) *Capturing the Evidence*. Leicester: National Youth Agency.

Pring, R. (2005) *Learning: Content, Quality, Assessment and Organisation*. Proceedings of the Nuffield Review. www.nuffield14-19review.org.uk.

Social Exclusion Unit (2005) *Transitions: Young Adults with Complex Needs*. London: The Stationery Office. Also, http://www.socialexclusionunit.gov.uk/downloaddoc.asp?id=785

Renouf, A., Griffin, C., Hitchings, L. and Riley, N. (2005) *Hear by Right: Building Standards for the active Involvement of children and young people*. Leicester: National Youth Agency.

Wylie, T. (2005) quoted in *ysqm framework for excellent services for young people*. Leicester: National Youth Agency.

Appendix 1: The history of detached youth work

For an in-depth bibliography of related texts, see http://www.infed.org/youthwork/b-detyw.htm and, in particular:

Cox, D. (1970) *A Community Approach to Youth Work in East London*. London: Young Women's Christian Association.

Goetschius, G.W. and Tash, J. (1967) *Working with Unattached Youth: Problem, Approach and Method*. London: Routledge and Kegan Paul.

Morse, M. (1965) *The Unattached*. Harmondsworth: Penguin.

Wild, J. (1982) *Streetmates*. Liverpool, Merseyside Youth Association.

Appendix 2: Key Guidelines and Standards for Excellence.

Guidelines

- Agencies need a clear statement of **aims** and **values**. This should inform **objectives** and anticipated outcomes. All staff should be familiar with this material and ensure that it informs their **practice, professional development** and the **identity** of the project.

- All stakeholders must be supported in developing an understanding of what detached youth work is [and also what it is not] and the contribution it can make. Reflecting on definitions is an essential part of this.

- A strong and coherent **vision** of what detached youth work is must be asserted. In particular, this should emphasise its **educational focus** and role in **engaging young people who are not accessing mainstream services**.

- The activities of workers should cohere with their **job descriptions** to ensure that their work reflects this vision and not that of a different agency.

- Detached youth work must be employed as an **appropriate** response rather than a default position. As such, its use should be informed by a thorough **assessment** of young people's needs and checked against a comprehensive and on-going **community profile**.

- Service levels need to emphasise quality rather than quantity.

- Work should focus on a single, specific, spatially defined community, or **'patch'**.

- **Community development** and **networking** activities should be resourced.

- Targeting individuals should be avoided and **voluntary association** respected. This does not preclude working with individuals identified by other agencies, provided this is in the context of detached youth work, where offers of individual support emerge from the voluntary context.

- An **access audit** should be employed to inform a practical commitment to **equality of opportunity**.

- Agencies should plan for **'fit'** between detached youth work and other forms of provision and **refer**, as appropriate.

- **Initial contacts** should be street rather than institution-based. They should not be prescriptive, i.e. they should reflect an approach in which an initial lack of structure supports negotiation of a more structured programme thereafter.

- Practice should emphasise **communication skills** and the development of strong **relationships**. Programmes should be enduring in order to provide **time** for this to happen, but **scrutinise effectiveness** and change focus as necessary.

- Practice and management should have democratic credentials and be highly **participative**. **Self-advocacy** and **autonomy** should be promoted.

- Opportunities for **reflection** and **analysis** should be resourced with time, supervision and training.

- **Monitoring** should, in the initial stages, be minimal and, if necessary to support relationship building, be purely observation-based. It should never be obtrusive.

- The recording of **outcomes** should focus on benefit to young people, who should be central to the process of **evaluation**.

- **Accreditation** should be regarded as a possibility and not a prescribed outcome.

- Target-setting should be informed by the participation of young people.

- **Evidence-based practice** and 'what works' should be emphasised. **Assessment** should focus on learning.

- **Promotion** should be community rather than marketing oriented and prioritise efforts to develop a wider understanding of detached youth work among all partners and stakeholders.

- Projects should have well-resourced **infrastructure**, an independently identifiable **base** and dedicated **administrative support**.

- Projects should, wherever possible, be **core-funded**.

- **Management** should maintain a focus on supporting practice by engaging with it. Learning from this should inform negotiations with **partnerships**, especially where other forms of 'detached work' (c.f. detached *youth* work) are taking place; roles need to be clarified.

- **Part-time staffing** should be substantive in order to facilitate strong relationships with young people and provide opportunities for **training** and **professional development**.

Standards.
- **Minimum staffing resources should be one full-time, professionally trained, detached youth worker and two, locally trained part-timers, each working a minimum of three sessions per week.**

- **Projects should be funded for a minimum of two years.**

- **Contact with young people should be based on a minimum of two sessions per week entitlement.**

- **Detached youth workers should have access to generic, specialist and on-going issue-based training.**